HIDDEN TREASURES REVEALED

TEACHING THE JEWISH ROOTS OF THE CHRISTIAN FAITH
PART 2

BY

JOHN F. PHELPS

©2018 by Diann Ray Phelps. Published by *haOr l'Olam Ministry* of the Cumberland Presbyterian Church. All rights are reserved. No part of this book may be reproduced or transmitted except by written permission of the copyright holder. For permission contact *haOr l'Olam Ministry*, 4743 Happy Hollow Rd. Hawesville, KY 42348

©Shannon Wirrenga illustrations (pages xiii & 45) are used by permission. If you are interested in Shannon's artwork, contact her at swirrenga.art@bis.midco.net

©Ethan McCoy cover photograph is used by permission. You can contact Ethan at ethan.a.mccoy@gmail.com

Compiled by DIANN RAY PHELPS
Edited by SARAH WILBORN MCCOY

haOr l'Olam ministry
4743 Happy Hollow Rd.
Hawesville, KY 42348

Phone: 270-927-9835
E mail: diannphelps@icloud.com
Webpage: www.haorlolamministry.org

ISBN: 978-1796317428

TABLE OF CONTENTS

FORWARD v
ACKNOWLEDGEMENT vii
PREFACE ix
INTRODUCTION xi
SEEKING TO UNDERSTAND 1
   SOUNDING THE TRUMPET 1
   THE SECOND TEMPLE PERIOD 5
   ANGELS 10
   LOOKING CLOSELY 14
DIGGING DEEPER 18
   THE KINGDOM OF HEAVEN 18
   JESUS AND THE KINGDOM 25
   THE BREAKER PASSAGE 30
SEARCHING 38
   THE FIRST CENTURY 38
   SALVATION 42
   HOW JESUS SAW SALVATION 47
   WORK OUT OUR SALVATION 50
   ZACCHAEUS 54
   THE LOVING FATHER 58
FIRST CENTURY TOOLS 63
   JESUS' SOURCES 63
   THE GOLDEN RULE 67
   STYLE OF INTERPRETATION 68
THE RELIGIOUS STRUCTURE 75
   SECTS OF JUDAISM 75
   A DISCIPLE 82

- **DIFFICULT TEACHINGS** 87
  - DEAD BURY THE DEAD 87
  - CURSING THE FIG TREE 93
  - HYPROCRITES 98
- **THE HEART OF IT ALL** 101
  - JESUS' HEART 101
  - RESTORING BROKEN RELATIONSHIPS 102
  - BORN FROM ABOVE 103
  - MORE PEACE, MORE JOY, MORE LOVE 105
  - GOD'S PEACE 107
- **BACK TO THE KINGDOM** 110
  - IN THE GARDEN 110
  - WHERE ARE YOU 117
  - MAN'S RULE 120
  - KINDS OF POWER 122
- **GOD'S PLAN** 126
  - RECONCILED 126
  - THE LORD'S PRAYER 132
  - I WILL BUILD MY CHURCH 134
  - HIS GOOD NEWS 136
- **THE GREAT COMMANDMENT** 140
  - BE MY DISCIPLES 140
  - SH'MA 144
  - YOU SHALL LOVE 148
  - ALL YOUR HEART 151
  - ALL YOUR SOUL 153
  - ALL YOUR STRENGTH 155
  - LOVE YOUR NEIGHBOR 156
- **SELECTED BIBLIOGRAPHY** 162
- **INDEX** 166

FORWARD

What a joy to be given the privilege to review the second volume in a collection of writings by a friend and colleague truly absorbed by the subject matter! The late Rev. John Phelps was a faithful minister of the Lord Jesus Christ, and served in the Cumberland Presbyterian Church until his death in 2008. The son of a minister himself, his father served my home church when I was very young. Years later when we were both grown, at various gatherings, he would often rush up to me and tell anyone around that he could still remember when I was very young! He confessed to me after one such occasion, apologetically explaining that as the son of a minister who served many churches, someone was always reminding him of his childhood! This remembrance is now a cherished memory of our friendship.

As John explains at the outset of this volume, the second in a planned series, it was a wish of his to arrange his studies in the connection between Judaism and Christianity, and to do so for a general audience. His beloved wife, Diann picked up the mantle, and with the assistance of family, continues to compile these articles into a coherent (stringing together) unit which illustrates John's industrious studies and clear discussion of otherwise little known aspects of the New Testament seen within a context of Second Temple Judaism.

His expositions are clear and accessible, and he certainly achieves his desired end of showing how an understanding of Judaic teaching and understanding of its influence upon Jesus and other leaders in the New Testament community. Numerous passages of Scripture which seem opaque come to light when the Jewish background is explained and illustrated. His writing enlightens and charms, even when discussing issues which most folks would not have *anticipated or expected—perhaps thinking they already understood certain passages and images.*

I found his discussion of the Breaker passage pp. 30-37 particularly enlightening. The anecdote about basketball on pp. 57-58 was also helpful. I don't believe that I had ever seen the number of Jewish sects in the New Testament era totaling 20 (p. 75)! The final chapter served as a wonderful summation of the insights and enhanced understanding of the Jewish flavor of the New Testament.

It is rewarding to see this volume being made available, knowing that it will be an invaluable aid to all who wish to gain a more comprehensive understanding of the teachings of Jesus and his followers. I commend it highly to all those who wish to deepen not only their awareness of the influence of the Old Testament on the New Testament, but even more, deepen their faith in and obedience to Almighty God.

Rev. Dr. David Lancaster ~ (B. A. - Bethel U; M.Div. - Yale Divinity School; D. Min. - Graduate Theological Union); Cumberland Presbyterian Pastor: Milburn Chapel Church, West Paducah. KY (1980-85); Knoxville First Church, Knoxville, TN (1985-2004); Professor: Bethel University, Old Testament Studies (2004-present); Program of Alternate Studies (1986-2018)

ACKNOWLEDGEMENT

First and foremost, I want to thank the LORD for His guidance and direction as I attempted a nearly impossible task for me. You see, I am dyslexic, and thus I am not a reader. This project has definitely stretched me way past my comfort zone. Also, I so appreciate John for his great love of the LORD, his zeal to be an essential part of maturing the Bride, and for leaving behind a well-spring of materials. He began taping his messages in 1986, at my mother's encouragement. When we began *'haOr l'Olam Ministry,'* he continued taping. It would truly take me another lifetime to transform all of his teachings and sermons into written format.

Second, I want to thank our granddaughter, Sarah Wilborn McCoy, for her hard work and editing skills; Rev. Dr. David Lancaster for his kind words in the forward; Shannon Wirrenga for sharing her art work with us; Ethan McCoy, our grandson-in-law, for capturing my vision for the cover page; our grandson, Joshua Wilborn, for his patience while being photographed for the cover page; and our grandson, Dustin Phelps, for computer assistance.

I want to thank all those that were my go-to sources when I was stuck: David Bivin and Clif Payne are both Jewish Roots scholars and were able to help me find references to several of John's quotes; our daughter, Kim Wilborn, for the many times she looked up scriptures for me, and for believing in me through this arduous project; and Phillip Layne for his help in the area of historical facts, and being a great support.

Last but not least, I want to thank Beth El Shaddai for their support of our ministry, both through prayer and financially for so many years. Without their financial support, I would not have been able to continue the ministry, much less published John's teachings. I also want to thank all those that opened their pulpits and gave John the opportunity to share the message, and for those that have donated to the ministry.

~ Diann Ray Phelps

PREFACE

This is the second half of *Hidden Treasures Revealed*. There was just too much information for one book, thus it was necessary to divide it into Part 1 and Part 2. Like *Hidden Treasures Revealed* Part 1, this book is made up of the teaching of Rev. John F. Phelps, compiled from his notes and many recorded teachings. Part 1 Preface contains Johns testimony. We chose not to include it in part 2, but we do hope you will take the time to read it.

John's goal in teaching of the Hebrew Roots of the Christian faith was to increase our understanding of the Holy Scriptures, to help us rediscover our purpose, identity, our mission in life, and to ultimately love God more!

You might ask, "is this study important?" The Christian faith was birthed out of Judaism. Jesus taught in a Jewish setting as a Rabbi of the first century A.D. It is difficult to understand His sayings and method without having some understanding of the culture in which He lived and taught. The same is true of Paul. The meanings of many of the sayings which are important to believers today are concealed by culture and/or language. Unlocking these for our understanding are important to our ability to do the word as we are commanded.

Studying our Hebrew heritage is not an attempt to make us Jewish or to put us under the Law. What he strived to do was to paint a more complete picture of Yeshua (Jesus), our Messiah's (Christ) vision for His body. John's goal was to see the church rediscover its identity, purpose and mission.

This book starts out with some foundational principles, then delves into some of John's favorite teachings: Jesus' understand of salvation, the great commandment, and an in-depth review on Jesus' understanding of the Kingdom.

This book is written the way John taught. For you who heard John teach, I pray you can hear him in this presentation. It is impossible to capture the zeal with which John delivered these teachings, but hopefully the nuggets of truth he discovered will be a blessing to you.

~ *Diann Ray Phelps*

INTRODUCTION

This is a direct quote from John before he began each Jewish Roots teaching:

"I want you to gain three things from these teachings:

Number one, I want you to gain an appreciation that there is more in the Scripture than you have seen before, and that there are rich treasures to be found once we learn when and where and how to dig.

Number two, I want you to become familiar with resources

that you can turn to, places you can go for information, for background studies, to find what you need when you need it. None of us carry all of the information in ourselves and no one source has all the answers. So, number one is an appreciation that there is more in the text than we have seen. Number two is knowing where to look to begin to open up those doors.

*Number three, this is the most important one of all, to let the text impact us so suddenly we say: "You mean this is what God expects of me, and this is what I need to do?" In other words, if this teaching does not somehow show us how God wants us to respond to Him, then we haven't really grown. If all we have gained is information and knowledge, I have failed to reach my goal for you and this teaching. I want ultimately for these teachings to result in you being either a better student of the Bible, or **more deeply in love with Jesus** than ever before, or a **better witness** of your faith than ever before.*

Whether it is a formal setting or private setting, my goal is for you to be able to counter some of the lies of the enemy, for you to be able to have some information that can be shared with others and see them become excited about the word of God. It's more than trivia, it is something that impacts our lives. So these are the goals that we're shooting for."

In His Service,

John F. Phelps

John F. Phelps

Let us be as clay in the POTTERS Hands. LORD, mold us and make us after YOUR will! Amen!

Sounding the Trumpet

CHAPTER ONE

SEEKING TO UNDERSTAND

SOUNDING THE TRUMPET

In this teaching, I will repeat many things we have gone over before, but remember, repetition is the price of learning. Jesus taught certain theological ideas in a different way than we are normally taught today. This is primarily because Jesus presented His subject in a way that the people of His time would understand, using examples from the customs and culture of that day. When Scriptures are interpreted according to modern culture, we miss so much of the meaning of His words. For me, that just doesn't work.

An example that I believe to be a mistranslation is found in Matthew 6:2, *"When you give alms* (charitable offering), *do not sound the trumpet as the hypocrites do in the Synagogues and in the street, that they may have glory from men. Assuredly I say to you, they have their reward."* What is Jesus saying here? This verse shows elements of being tampered with. "In the Synagogues and in the streets;" we need to understand that people did not bring money to Synagogues. Money was and is not handled in the Synagogue on the Sabbath, thus they didn't take up an offering.[1] There were beggars in the streets, and alms were given to them there. What about "sound the trumpet?" Sounding the trumpet was a

---

[1] Abraham Cohen, *Everyman's Talmud: The Major Teachings of the Rabbinic Sages* (New York, NY: Schocken, 1995), p. 221.

known term from Jewish writings.

Let's look at the Second Temple Period and the customs of that day to help us understand this statement. The whole area of the Temple was called the Temple Complex, and there were various courts.

One of these courts was the Court of Prayer were thirteen boxes for collecting offerings were located. Each box was marked how the money would be used. Seven offering boxes were designated as temple dues and required offerings.[2] The other six were offerings ranged from giving at the birth of a child to someone who had been declared clean. There was also a free will offering, called Alms Box, for the poor.[3] There was a secret society for the distributing the offerings to the needy. That way, the poor did not feel obligated to a certain person, and the person giving it did not feel superior to the person receiving it. Given anonymously was known as "charitable deeds."[4]

The fact is, the boxes were made of brass and shaped large at the bottom like a bell with a narrow neck to discourage thievery. Because of the shape of the offering boxes, they were called "the trumpets;" the thirteen offering "trumpets."[5] What I believe the text is supposed to say is, "They sound the trumpet when they stand in the corner." When they came into the corner of the Temple where the Alms Boxes were, there were people all around and they were supposed to be giving

---

[2] Alec Garrard, *The Splendor of the Temple* (Grand Rapids, MI: Kregel Publications, 2001), p. 66.
[3] Ibid., p. 67.
[4] Alfred Edersheim, *The Temple: Its Ministry and Services, as They Were at the Time of Jesus* (London: The Religious Tract Society, 1881), p. 49.
[5] Garrard, *Splendor of the Temple*, p. 66-67.

an anonymous gift, right?

What do you think it mean by sounding the trumpet? I believe they went to the offering box and dropping each coin in, *Clink! Clink! Clink!* This was known as "sounding the trumpet!"[6] In other words, they were calling attention to themselves by making the trumpet sound when they dropped their coins in. The anonymous donation was no longer anonymous. It was given for the praise of men and Jesus said that's exactly all they will get. *"Assuredly, I say to you, they have their reward."* [Matt. 6:2]

The Scripture might make us think that there was someone actually blowing the trumpet and saying, "Look at this huge gift I am giving!" The Scripture states, " *in the street."* There were street beggars and when they were given alms, it was not an anonymous gift. So, this really doesn't have any meaning in the context when relating to giving in the streets. Anyone giving a gift in the streets would have been seen by others. Peter and John, on their way to the Temple, encountered a street beggar asking for alms. *"Peter said, 'Silver and gold I do not have, but what I do have I give you: In the name of Jesus Christ of Nazareth, rise up and walk.'"* [Acts 3:6]

I feel sure that when the translators came to the word "corner," they assumed it was implying "street corner," because that's where beggars would be: by the gates and on the street corners. When we look at verse 5, we see *"hypocrites…pray standing in the Synagogues and on the corners of the streets."* [Matt. 6:5] I believe these two Scriptures were put together because of the mention of

---

[6] See "The Alms-Boxes" at
http://www.jewishencyclopedia.com/articles/1295-alms.

Synagogues and corners. Matthew 6:5 is the beginning of what we call the LORD's prayer. Luke 11:1 has His disciples asking Jesus to *"teach us to pray, as John also taught his disciples."* Luke does not mention "hypocrites," "Synagogues," or "corners."

In Matthew 6:2, I truly believe the writer intended it to say the "corner" referring to the area in the Temple where the offering boxes were located. Knowing the Jewish understanding of the Alms Boxes as "trumpets" changes our view of this Scripture. Jesus went on to say, *"Do not let your left hand know what your right hand is doing."* [Matt. 6:3] This was a rabbinical way of saying, "Give in secret." Let God be the judge of what we give, and give because there is a need to give and a desire to help others. Do not give to receive praise from man, but give because of your love for God.

There was a specific court called the Court of the Gentiles. This was set aside for people who believed in God, but chose not to convert to Judaism. They were known as the "God fearers." They were allowed to come as far as the Court of the Gentiles, but they could go no further. There were signs placed at frequent intervals in Greek and Latin forbidding gentiles "pass this point on pain of death!" One of these signs has been recovered.[7] In Acts 21:38, Paul was accused of taking a non-Jew past that wall.

During the Second Temple period there was an area called the Holy Precinct where the Israelites gathered. The original Tabernacle and Temple of Solomon consisted of the Holy of Holies, the Holy

---

[7] See "The Gates" at www.jewishencyclopedia.com/articles/14304-temple-of-Herod.

Place, and an area of sacrifice called the Court of the Priests. An additional court was added to the Second Temple which was called the Court of the Unclean. This court was where they came to be declared clean. Guess who was unclean more than anyone? The women were, because of their monthly cycle and childbirth. Therefore, it came to be known as the Court of the Women or the Women's Court, but originally it was the Court of the Unclean.[8]

THE SECOND TEMPLE PERIOD

Since we have been discussing the Second Temple, let's delve deeper into some facts concerning this period in Jewish history. As we continue our study to increase our understanding of the Bible, we need to have at least a working knowledge of the Second Temple Period. We need to understand their customs as well as their beliefs and practices.

Why is that time period so important? That time frame brackets the birth, life, and death of Jesus! *Yeshua*, Jesus, came as a Jew, thus Christianity was birthed out of Judaism of that time. So, if we want to understand Christianity better, we need to understand Judaism of the Second Temple Period.

When the Temple was destroyed in 70 A.D., only

---

[8] Merrill C. Tenney, *The Zondervan Pictorial Dictionary*, 25th ed. (Grand Rapids: Zondervan, 1963), p. 835.

two sects of Judaism survived: the Pharisees and the *ma'aminim*, Hebrew for "The Believers." In Acts 9:2, Paul refers to them as people *"who were of the Way."* Jews called them *Natzratim* or *Notzrim* which identified them as one of the Jewish sects of the time.[9] It is accepted among scholars that "at the end of the First Century, there were not yet two separate religions called 'Judaism' and 'Christianity.'"[10]

Judaism of today is the descendant of the Pharisees, and today's Christianity is the descendant of *ma'aminim*. Both Christianity and Judaism of today were birthed out of that same period; the same Birth Mother, "twins in the womb and sharing the same spiritual food." The Birth Mother puts her imprint and characteristic on her child, and we have that imprint. That is why I say that Judaism is really a brother to Christianity. Since the Pharisees came along first, they are the elder brother and we are the younger brother. We were both birthed out of the Second Temple Period. Christianity is the descendant of the Jews of the Second Temple Period that accepted Jesus as their Messiah.[11]

What is the Second Temple Period? Let me share a little history here. Jewish history is basically divided between the First Temple Period which begins with Solomon who constructed the first Temple. Solomon became king in 971 B.C. and began construction of the First Temple almost immediately. It took seven years to

---

[9] David H. Stern, *Jewish New Testament Commentary: A Companion Volume to the Jewish New Testament* (Clarksville, MD: Jewish New Testament Publications, 1992), p. 253; Acts 9:1-2.
[10] Robert Goldenberg, *The Jewish Quarterly Review* 92, no. ¾ (2002): 568-88.
[11] Stern, *Jewish NT Commentary*, p. 228; Acts 2:46-47.

build. The Temple was built on Mount Moriah and that Temple stood until the year 586 B.C.[12]

In 586 B.C. Nebuchadnezzar destroyed the First Temple and took all the Temple treasures to Babylon. [Jer. 39:5-8] This time period was referred to as the Babylonian Captivity. After King Solomon's death, the northern kingdom divided from the southern kingdom in 931 B.C. The northern kingdom was destroyed by the Assyrians in 722 B.C. and Samaria fell. All that was left was Judah (Judea as it was later called). Later under Ezra, Zerubbabel, and Jeshua, the rebuilding of the Temple began. This Temple was the beginning of the Second Temple Period. The rebuilt Temple was a poor representation of the original Temple. How do we know this? By reading our Scripture closely, it tells us that the *"old men who had seen the first Temple wept,"* because it was a far cry from the splendor of Solomon's Temple. [Ezra 3:12]

The Second Temple Period, from the very first construction to destruction, was from 515 B.C. to 70 A.D. Some say the Second Temple period began when Herod agreed to the expansion, but it really began with the rebuilding of the Temple under Zerubbabel. Antiochus Epiphanies despised the Jews so much, he desecrated the Temple by forcing the High Priest to sacrifice swine on the altar, which was called the

---

[12] "B.C." stands for "Before Christ" and "A.D." stands for *Anno Domini* which is Latin for "in the year of our LORD." The B.C. and A.D. system was devised in 525 A.D. but was not widely used until the nineteenth century. Incidentally, we know that our calendar is off anywhere from three to six years. For an example, instead of the year 2017, the year could be anywhere from 2020 to 2023.

"abomination of desolation."[13] The Maccabean Revolt that took place in 168 B.C. defeated the Assyrians and Antiochus, and resulted in the reclaiming of the Temple

The Israel Museum in Jerusalem's to-scale model of the Second Temple.

The priest rededicated the Temple at that time and the celebration of *Chanukah* was established to remember the cleansing of the Temple and the miracle God preformed.[14]

Under the Maccabean rule, Israel gained full control of their country. After the victory, the temple was cleansed and re-dedicated. [15] They began expanding the Temple to the south, enlarged the Temple's platform, and took out the Assyrian quarters that were to the south of the original Solomon's Temple

---

[13] Daniel 9:27, 11:31, 12:11; Matthew 24:15; Mark 13:14; Luke 21:12
[14] Michael Strassfield, *The Jewish Holidays: A Guide and Commentary* (New York: Harper & Row, 1985), p. 161-163.
[15] I Maccabees 4:36-59

wall.[16]

The best drawing of the Second Temple after Herod the Great's massive building program that I have seen was done by Martha Ritmeyer.

Herod expanded the Temple to the north and south. This whole complex was 1,600 by 900 English feet, nine stories high and walls up to sixteen feet thick. I truly feel it should have been included as one of the seven wonders of the ancient world. It was big enough to hold over 30 football fields and could accommodate hundreds of thousands of people at any given time. It was magnificent in all its splendor. This was the Temple that Jesus spent His time in and where He went to as a boy.[17] This is where Jesus went for the God ordained pilgrim Festivals: Passover, Pentecost or *Sukkot*.

Jesus said in Matthew 24:2, *"Not one stone shall be left here upon another."* Jesus said the Temple would be destroyed *"and in three days I will raise it up."* They answered Jesus, *"It has taken 46 years to build this Temple."* [John 2:19-20] They were speaking of the expansion of Herod, and the construction had not been completed.

That was how massive this Temple was. This was the time of the great Rabbis such as Rabbi Hillel and Rabbi Shammai.[18] Jesus came right in the middle of all that richness! This was also the Temple during the time of Paul and the early Church.

The Romans Emperor Vespasian started a

---

[16] For more information see http://www.jewishencyclopedia.com/articles/14304-temple-of-herod.
[17] Luke 2:41-45
[18] Ron Moseley, *Yeshua: A Guide to the Real Jesus and Original Church* (Clarksville, MD: Messianic Jewish Publishers, 1998), p. 155-156.

campaign against the Jews, and his son, Emperor Titus, who succeeded his father, finished the job of destroying the Temple in 70 A.D.[19] The Temple was completely destroyed and it has never been rebuilt. When we visit Israel, we see the remains of the Second Temple. The Jews today pray at the West wall of the Temple Mount, known as the Wailing Wall. Visitors from all over the world, Christians and Jews alike, come to the Wailing Wall to pray and put their prayer request in the cracks of the wall.

ANGELS

Let's look at another example of why we need to know the culture of Jesus' time. A common misconception is found in Revelation 2:1, *"To the angel of the church at Ephesus write..."* This one is very simple because we find it throughout Jewish writings.[20] They talk about the Angel of the Synagogue. Now, what does it mean? The word "angel" is *angelos* in Greek and *mal'ak* in Hebrew. They both literally mean "messenger." Think about it: what did God's angels primarily do in the New Testament? They brought messages. Let's put the word messenger in and read it. "To the messenger of the church...write." Does that make sense? Write to the one who gives the message, or

---

[19] Garrard, *Splendor of the Temple*, p. 5.
[20] John Lightfoot, *A Commentary on the New Testament from the Talmud and Hebraica: Matthew- 1 Corinthians*, Vol. 2 (Grand Rapids: Baker Book House, 1979), p. 90.

the worship director. So, what is Jesus telling John to do? "Write this letter to the one that will read it to the congregation."

These were real letters to real churches, to be read by the worship leader to the congregation. Yes, the letters have implications for the churches down through history. As with all Scripture, it has implications far beyond the surface meaning. With this small adjustment, we see that the "angel of the church" was not a spiritual being. They were the leaders of that congregation. Not necessarily the one who delivered the message. In most cases the head Elder was the teacher of the congregation. The announcer was the one that directed worship.

Jesus is instructing John to have the worship leader read the letter to the Church. In verse 8, Jesus said, *"I am the Alpha and the Omega, the Beginning and the End."* We know that this was written in Greek, because of the use of Alpha and Omega. This makes since because the letters were written to Greek churches. Revelation is highly symbolic in all of its language, so it is easy to understand why the reference to angels could be misunderstood.

For example, note all the repetition of sevens throughout the Book of Revelation. There are the seven bowls, the seven angels, the seven stars, the seven seals, the seven churches, the seven years, and the seven Spirits of God. In Hebrew *shaba* is a primitive root word and the base word for seven.[21] We see *shaba* in Genesis 2:2, "and on the seventh day God rested." Do you see

---

[21] James Strong, *The Exhaustive Concordance of the Bible* (Cincinatti: Jennings & Graham, 1890), p. 136; Hebrew word #7650, #7651.

shaba in *Shabbat*? Seven is important throughout Scripture.

Furthermore, when we read Revelation, we need to remember that these are not the words of John, but it is Jesus' revelation, and John is the recipient of the word. Now, the chosen ones, the selected ones, God has put these people in their places for a specific reason, as He did the stars in the heavens.

Since we are talking about the "angel of the church," let's look at the heavenly beings that are known as angels. What does Scripture tell us about these celestial beings? They are first mentioned in Genesis 3:24, when God drove Adam and Eve from the garden. God put cherubim with flaming swords to guard the entrance to the garden.

"The Mercy Seat"

The Hebrew word for cherubim is *keruvim*. The word is plural and many believe that *keruvim* means "*covering angels.*"²² God instructed Moses to "*make two cherubim of gold… of the mercy seat.*" [Exod. 25:18] This was the lid of the Ark of the Covenant. In Ezekiel 10, Ezekiel describes his vision of cherubim.

We often see statues of babies with wings that are called Cherub, not to be confused with Cherubim.. Nothing in Scripture supports a naked, plump winged baby concept. This image came from the Greco-Roman deity known as Cupid or Eros, a pagan god.²³

The next celestial being I want to mention is found in Isaiah 6. "*I saw the LORD sitting on a throne, high and lifted up, and the train of His robe filled the temple. Above it stood seraphim; each one had six wings: with two he covered his face, with two he covered his feet, and with two he flew.*" To me this is an awesome passage: the call of Isaiah. Obviously, the job of the seraphim is to minister to the LORD in worship; praising, glorify, and serving Him.

Besides the cherubim and seraphim, angels are mentioned almost 300 times from Genesis through Revelation. They have specific jobs they do for God. We, as Christians, are most familiar with the angelic messenger, Gabriel, who appeared to Mary and Joseph. The Shepherds also experienced angelic visitation, but the angels were not named. In Daniel 9 and 10, the Scripture tells us that Daniel prayed fervently. In 10:2 it says that he "*was mourning for three full weeks.*" In this angelic encounter, Daniel is told that his prayers were heard the first day, but the demonic ruler over "*Persia withstood me twenty-one days.*" Daniel 10: 13 goes on to say that "*Michael, one of the chief princes, came to help me.*"

---

²² See "Word Wealth" in Nelson *NKJV Spirit Filled Bible*, p. 118.
²³ Isidore, Etymolgiae, 8.11.80

Michael is described as an archangel in Jude 9, where he is disputing with Satan over the body of Moses.[24] He is also found in Revelation 12:7-9 fighting the dragon. Angelic beings are mighty and powerful beings; they are sent by God to do a specific task and to hold back the enemy so that God's work can be done on earth.

    I believe that when we pray earnestly, God sends His angels to move those mountains in our lives and the lives of those we are praying for. Let me share what I consider a perfect example. My cousin, Rev. Buddy Stott, a missionary to Japan for 27 years, told me that when the Women's Missionary Auxiliary changed their emphasis from fervently supporting the missionaries in prayer, he could feel the difference because of the lack of prayer cover. When the saints of the LORD are on their knees; souls are won, lives are changed, and ministries flourish.

LOOKING CLOSELY

    If there is one thing I have learned through my many years of preaching and teaching, it is that some topics are taboo. These concepts are so ingrained in the Christian way of thinking, that even when presented with facts to the contrary, the old ideas keep creeping back in. Well, we will be going into some of those taboo areas. I am going to endeavor to challenge you to open your minds to some new concepts. They do not

---

[24] Moseley, *Yeshua*, p. 150-152.

challenge our faith in Jesus as our Messiah. Hopefully, they just expand our understanding. I have said, from the beginning, that we need to read our Bibles like detectives, and that is what I want us to do.

Let's look at some common misconceptions that most of us hold dear. First, how many wise men traveled to Bethlehem? The Scripture doesn't say. Let's look closely at the second chapter of Matthew. It tells us what the gifts were, *"gold, frankincense, and myrrh,"* but it does not indicate if there were two, three, four or more wise men. One could have brought two gifts, or maybe some gifts were repeated. All we know for sure is that there were three types of gifts.

Where was the family when the wise men brought the gifts? Verse 11 states *"and when they had come into the house, they saw the young Child with Mary."* We see over and over again the nativity scene with baby Jesus, Mary, Joseph, the shepherds, and three wise men. Does this change the meaning of the story? No, but are we reading our Scriptures closely, or are we just going along with tradition?

What about the angels that appeared to the shepherds? Were the angels singing? Luke 2:13 says, *"And suddenly there was with the multitude of the heavenly host praising God and saying…"* Nothing says they were singing, but our tradition and songs have taught us that they were. I mention these Scriptures to demonstrate how our view can be influenced by tradition.

An easily misunderstood Scripture is found in Luke and Matthew. *"What you hear in the ears, preach on the housetops."* [Matt. 10:27] Luke 12:3 quotes Jesus, *"What you hear whispered in your ear, shout it from the roof tops."* Jesus was not saying to share things told in secret or to gossip. The Jewish people listening to Him heard and understood very clearly what He was saying, "From your mouth to my ear."

People living outside of the land of Israel did not necessarily understand Hebrew. Their Scriptures, which we call the Old Testament, were all written in Hebrew. The Septuagint had been developed. the Septuagint was the translation from Hebrew into Greek, but for the most part, the Hebrew text was used in their worship services, much like Latin was in the Roman Catholic Church for centuries. Thus, the people that were from outside of the land of Israel did not understand what was being read. The person reading the text would read it softly into the ear of an interpreter, He was called the *meturgenam*. [25] The interpreter would hear the word spoken softly in his ear and he would interpret it loudly for everyone to hear. He was not only proclaiming the Word of God, he was interpreting the Word and putting it into the language the people could understand. Thus, whatever was whispered in the ear, should not be kept secret, but proclaimed loudly for all to hear. So, what was Jesus saying? "Just like the interpreter who did the actual interpretation, let the Spirit of the LORD whisper in your ear, and you be the one who proclaims it loudly to everyone."

Let me share a personal example of a misconception I had. One Sunday my sermon topic was on Moses at Mt. Sinai. I felt secure in my facts, but I kept hearing "read the Scripture." Finally, I got out of bed and read the account in Exodus. To my amazement, my

---

[25] Moseley, *Yeshua*, p.5.

recollection had been greatly influenced by the movie *The Ten Commandments*. Our understanding of Scripture can be influenced by many experiences, from movies to what we were taught as children.

In this teaching, I will be challenging your understanding of such terms as "heaven" and "salvation." I want to delve into the understanding of how Jesus used these terms. For example, "heaven" was a substitute for the name of God, such as in Daniel 4:26, *"Your kingdom shall be assured to you, after you come to know Heaven rules."* This is a perfect example of circumlocution. Circumlocution is to talk around, or to use other words as a substitute. By the Second Temple Period, the Hebrews would not use God's Holy Name in fear of breaking the Third Commandment. They even stopped using the word "God" so as not to use it in an unholy way.[26]

---

[26] John Phelps, *Hidden Treasures Revealed: Teaching the Jewish Roots of the Christian Faith, Part One* 2016), p. 54-58.

CHAPTER TWO

DIGGING DEEPER

THE KINGDOM OF HEAVEN

We will now delve into the understanding of the kingdom of heaven and the Biblical presentation of it. From the Sermon on the Mount, Jesus says *"Blessed are the poor in spirit for theirs is the kingdom of heaven."* [Matt. 5:3] He goes on to say, *"Rejoice and be exceedingly glad, for great is your reward in heaven, for so they persecuted the prophets who were before you."* [Matt. 5:12] These are just two examples of the use of the word "heaven." What was Jesus saying when He spoke of "the kingdom of heaven?" When Jesus uses the word heaven, He was **not** referring to the same thing we commonly understand heaven to mean. For example, today how do most people view the word, "heaven?" They will define the term as the place we go after we die. Christians refer to it as our eternal dwelling place with God. But that is not how Jesus uses the word "heaven." The Hebrew word for heaven is *shamayim*; it refers to the sky, the abode of the stars, the atmosphere.

When a Jewish person of the first century talked about a place following death, they would either say, *"gathered to his people,"* *"rested with his fathers,"* *"the age to come,"* *"world to come,"* or *"Paradise."* [Gen. 49:33, 2 Chr. 9:31, Mark 10:30] Jesus said to the thief on the cross, *"Today you will be with Me in Paradise."* [Luke 23:42] What did He mean by Paradise? The Hebrew understanding of the word

Paradise was *Gan Eden*, or the Garden of Eden.[27] Another term that was used for where they would go when they died was *Sheol*. *Sheol*, *ádis* in Greek, was understood to hold the dead until the final judgment.[28] In other words, *Sheol* contained the place of Paradise and the place of torment. Paradise was also called "*Abraham's bosom.*" [Luke 16:22] Remember Lazarus and the rich man? I believe this is where Jesus went and preached to those who had died before His resurrection. [Eph. 4:8-9] During Jesus' time, they did not talk about going into the presence of God.

The place of punishment, hell, was called *Gey-Hinnom*, which referred to the valley of *Hinnom*, the garbage dump just outside the city walls.[29] They would pass through the Dung Gate to threw their trash into the *Hinnom* valley. The fires continually burned there, so this became symbolic of the place of torment where *"their worm does not die and the fire is not quenched."* [Mark 9:48] For those who accepted *Yeshua* as their *Messiah*, their understanding of *Ge Hinnom* changed after His resurrection. Paul stated that Jesus *"ascended on high, He led captivity captive."* [Eph. 4:8] So Paul was saying Jesus went to Paradise and preached to those who had died before His coming & led them to salvation.

"The age to come" or "the world to come," *Olam ha-Ba* in Hebrew, also carried with it a strong Messianic Age concept.[30] But whether they were talking about the end of the age or when one dies, they did not use the word "heaven." When Jesus used the term "heaven" or

---

[27] Stern, *Jewish NT Commentary*, p. 149; Luke 23:43.
[28] Ibid., p. 134; Luke 16:23.
[29] Ibid., p. 29; Matt. 5:22.
[30] David Flusser, *Jesus* (Reinbeck: Rowohlt, 1968), p. 110.

"the kingdom of heaven," He was not speaking of our eternal destination. So, what was He talking about? Earlier we discussed circumlocution, meaning to talk around a word.[31] The First Century Jew substituted other words for the name of God to avoid using the word "God." Why? To keep from breaking the third commandment; in fear of using it in a less than holy way. "Heaven" was a common substitute for God's holy name, *YHWH*, and even the word "God."

With this understanding in hand, when we see, "kingdom of heaven" in our Scriptures, we need to read "kingdom of God." Matthew was the only gospel that used the term "kingdom of heaven." This is because he was more Hebraic than the other gospels and so was his audience, thus Matthew used the circumlocution of "heaven." "Heaven" and "God" are really two different ways of saying the same thing.

Let's do some scripture comparison here. In Matthew 3:2, John the Baptist was preaching *"Repent, for the kingdom of heaven is at hand."* Now, let's look at Mark 1:15: *"The time is fulfilled, and the kingdom of God is at hand."* Do you see? These are the same statements, only phrased slightly differently. Mark was a scribe to Peter while Peter was in Rome speaking to Gentiles, thus Peter would have been free to use the term God with his audience. Matthew, on the other hand, was speaking to a Hebrew audience, so it would have been offensive to the Hebrew listeners for the word "God" to have been used. Luke's gospel is much more Greek in its presentation. He used the terms that his readers would understand because he needed to be more

---

[31] Phelps, *Hidden Treasures Revealed, Part 1*, p. 64-69.

straightforward with his audience. We see this in the very first statement of Luke's letter to Theophilus. He stated, *"to write to you an orderly account."* [Luke 1:3] As we mentioned earlier, the chronological order of things is very much a Greek way of thinking.[32]

The kingdom of God was the central theme in Jesus' teachings. In fact, not only did He teach this, He also told His disciples to teach *"the kingdom of heaven is at hand."* [Matt. 10:7] His instructions to His disciples were to *"heal the sick, cleanse the lepers, raise the dead,* and *cast out demons."* [Matt. 10:8] Doesn't this show us that Jesus was referring to the kingdom of God as being present, the here-and-now?

Luke 10:9 is translated *"The kingdom of God has come near."* The words "has come near" in Greek is *engiken* and implies "about to appear" or "almost here." This suggests that the kingdom is not here yet, but is coming soon. However, the Hebrew word that is equivalent to *engiken* is *karav,* which means "it is here; it has arrived."[33] *Karav* is always in the present tense.

Jesus said, *"The Kingdom of God is within you."* [Luke 17:20] Doesn't that explain the Kingdom of God clearly? It is where God is actively reigning over those who accept Him as King of their lives for the here-and-now, and the age to come. Since we know Jesus taught in Hebrew, what does this imply? **Jesus intended for the kingdom to break in on the physical world, changing lives and making a difference.**

With this understanding in hand, let's look at a scripture that has caused a lot of concern.

---

[32] Phelps, *Hidden Treasures Revealed, Part 1*, p. 9-12.
[33] David Bivin and Roy Blizzard, *Understanding the Difficult Words of Jesus* (Shippensburg, PA: Destiny Image Publishers, 1994), p. 62.

> "*Do you not know that the unrighteous will not inherit the kingdom of God? Do not be deceived. Neither fornicators, nor idolaters, nor adulterers, nor homosexuals, nor sodomites, nor thieves, nor covetous, nor drunkards, nor revilers, nor extortioners will inherit the kingdom of God.*" [1 Cor. 6:9-10]

Do you see? This is not talking about being allowed to go to what we consider heaven. This is stating that those that allow sin to rule in their lives are not a part of His kingdom. In other words, God is not King of their lives. They may accept Jesus as their savior, but not as LORD. I know this is possible, because I walked for almost twenty years in this state. I knew the saving grace of God, but I did not surrender my will to Him. Thank the LORD, He never gave up on me. I can tell you that the joy, peace, and happiness I found when I surrendered to His Lordship is so much greater than I could ever imagine. He is such an awesome God!

Now, I want to share something that I find interesting about the use of the word heaven. In Matthew 5:3 and 5:12, and other places in the New Testament, the word "heaven," *shamayim*, is plural. We know this because of the *'im'* ending. The word is literally "heavens." In other words, *"Our Father who art in heaven"* [Matt. 6:9] would be more accurately translated to "in the heavens." This shows us that it was conveying a *concept* rather than a specific location. The concept of heaven in the Hebraic mind was dimensional rather than locational. So what does "the heavens" convey? It is speaking of a God who dwells in the spiritual realms and who is above nature.

Jews understand seven levels of heaven.[34] To name a few, there is the level around Earth, where the stars and the moon are; this is the realm where the demonic and the angelic operate. Then there are the highest heavens where God is supreme. Does that sound familiar? *"Glory to God in the highest."* [Luke 2:14] This is saying that God is the highest of all; God has authority over everything. So, what this is suggesting is that "Our Father who is Supernatural, Our Father who is the Supreme One." We are not of our earthly father Abraham, but "Our Father who is in the heavenly, spiritual realm."

In Matthew 5:3, Jesus stated, *"Blessed are the poor in spirit, for theirs is the kingdom of heaven."* This is a bad translation. It really should read, "Blessed are the poor in spirit for of such is the kingdom of heaven." They are a part of the people that make up God's kingdom; they don't own it or possess it. Isaiah speaks *of "a contrite and humble spirit,"* meaning a spiritual attitude. [Isa. 57:12] Realize that most of the Beatitudes are talking about **attitudes**. *"Rejoice and be exceedingly glad for great is your reward in heaven."* [Matt. 5:12] This is saying "great is your reward in your **relationship with God**; in God's eyes." Matthew 6:19-20 states, *"Do not lay up for yourselves treasures on earth, where moth and rust destroy and where thieves break in and steal but lay up for yourselves treasures in heaven."* Here Matthew is saying our reward is with God, which begins with salvation and continues throughout eternity!

Matthew 6:21 does not support the concept of a treasure stored up in "our eternal life." It is talking

---

[34] Cohen, *Everyman's Talmud*, p. 30.

about strengthening and building our spiritual walk with God. A lot of people have been led to believe that they need to work for rewards in heaven, but scripture teaches that if we work for the praise, we have missed the goal.[35] When we work because of our love for God and mankind, the reward is there. The rewards are a by-product. If we work for the reward, our motivation is wrong because it is selfish and self-centered. When love of God is our motivator, it removes the greed and self-centeredness. So "great is your reward" in your relationship with God.'

Is it wrong to think of heaven as our eternal home? No, because heaven is truly dwelling in the spiritual realm and in the presence of God. In fact, when I preach a funeral or minister to a grieving family, I will continue to use the term "heaven." If it comforts, then it has accomplished its purpose.

To understand our Scripture better, we need to recognize what Jesus was saying. When we see the word "heaven," we need to remember it is a circumlocution for God. I know this may go against everything we have been taught, but we are seeking to find the truths in Scriptures and understand the message He has for us. As we build our relationship with God, we are truly making Him King of our lives.

This understanding of heaven gives us insight into many of Jesus' teachings. For instance, by writing, *"the kingdom of heaven is at hand,"* Matthew was talking about something that is in the spiritual dimension. [Matt. 3:2, 4:17, 10:7] He was saying the kingdom is right here, right now; it is within you, among you, and in your

---

[35] Matthew 6:1-21

midst. Jesus said, *"If you cast out demons with the finger of God, surely the kingdom of God has come upon you."* [Luke 11:20] This is saying that Jesus saw the kingdom as a present reality rather than a future destination. When we limit heaven to simply a future destination, we are missing the point of God's kingship in our lives![36]

JESUS AND THE KINGDOM

The question comes down to how did Jesus understand the kingdom? First, let me say that there is a present dimension and a future dimension. The present is that the kingdom is a "now reality." The future dimension will come in greater fullness when Jesus returns, either when we are in the presence of God without the difficulties of this physical body or when Jesus comes at the end of the age, when His kingdom comes in fullness. It is a concept for now, but it has greater fullness that is yet to come. The kingdom is both a present and a future reality.

Jesus' concept was that the kingdom of God is an active force in the world, energized by God. That means He saw it as doing something and not just existing. It is breaking into this world, into man's reality, into man's existence and dimension, with the power of God behind it. That is my general definition of the kingdom

---

[36] There is a theology called, 'Kingdom Now' and I cannot agree with their teachings. I am not referring to that movement when I say the Kingdom of God is for now. We are supposed to be God's people now, and He is our King.

of heaven/kingdom of God. It is an active force in the world, activated by God's power. Jesus then went on to define the kingdom of God in three ways.

<u>First, in the kingdom, God reigns among people who have chosen to obey Him</u>.[37] We can ask the question, "Is God totally sovereign, or does man have free will?" The answer is yes. That bothers the Greek thinking mind. God is totally sovereign but He chooses to withhold His sovereignty when it comes to man's ability and right to choose. He has given man free will. This is the theme throughout Scripture. In the parable of the Prodigal Son, the father did not force the son to stay home. Instead, he gave him the freedom, even to make the wrong choices. The theme of the law is relationship motivated by love. Love is given freely and must be responded to freely; love is a decision to value someone and to hold them in high esteem.

If love is forced, the response is not love. Jesus said to the rich young ruler, *"Go sell everything that you have and give it to the poor and come and follow Me."* [Matt. 19, Mark 10, Luke 18] The man walked away because he would not give up his position and great possessions. Jesus didn't run after him and say, "Let's talk about this," because Jesus had to give him the freedom to make his own decision. Love requires that. 1 John 4:16 tells us *"God is love,"* thus it requires that the one created in His image has the freedom to choose. Jesus understood God's kingdom as God reigning and ruling over those that have chosen to love and obey Him. God invites everyone to become part of His kingdom.

---

[37] Brad H. Young, *Jesus the Jewish Theologian* (Grand Rapids, MI: Baker Publishing Group, 1993), p. 80.

Second, in the kingdom, God's power is manifested in the redemptive purposes of healing, deliverance, and salvation.[38] This is proof that the kingdom of God is present and His power is at work in people's lives. Wherever God's power breaks out, wherever the miraculous occurs, that is God's kingdom! That's why Jesus said, *"If I cast out demons by the Spirit of God, surely the kingdom of God has come upon you."* [Matt. 12:28] He took authority over the demonic realm. That is the miraculous occurring! It's God's power breaking in and establishing authority over the realm of the demonic. So, wherever we see God's power manifest, then the kingdom of God is at work.

Third, Jesus calls His movement the kingdom of God. He saw the people that accepted Him as Messiah bringing redemption to the world.[39] He calls His followers the kingdom of God! When Jesus was talking to Nicodemus, He said that he "cannot enter the kingdom of God," meaning, to become one of His followers. In John 3:5, Jesus tells Nicodemus that he must first have a spiritual birth, or it could also be translated a "rebirth." It is not a birth in the flesh, but a birth of the Spirit. Jesus was saying that one cannot be part of His movement, the kingdom, without a rebirth. And this is still true today.

In the first definition of the kingdom, when God is King, then His followers chose to obey Him and they are under His authority. Because of this, Jesus' followers were going to start being manifest, showing evidence of God's presence and power in their lives.

---

[38] Brad H. Young, *Jesus the Jewish Theologian* p. 81.
[39] Ibid. p. 81.

Whenever Jesus' disciples went out in His name, His power was made manifest: the sick were healed, demons were cast out, lives were changed, and souls were saved. This is what Jesus expects to see all His followers do; this is the kingdom of God.

It is sad to say, but when we look at the church of today, we should ask, where is the power? We must go back to the main requirement: God must be number one in our lives. That's the bottom line. So, if we want to see the power manifest through us, we must have this in place first. Jesus understood that this would be true of His movement, and of the people that followed Him. If they were going to be His followers, they were going to have to be obedient to God. When we are obedient to God, He is free to work through us, and only then can His glory shine through.

Many times, I have been told that certain sins will keep people out of heaven. They quote 1st Corinthians 6:9-10:

> *"Do you not know that the unrighteous will not inherit the kingdom of God? Do not be deceived. Neither fornicators, nor idolaters, nor adulterers, nor homosexuals, nor sodomites, nor thieves, nor covetous, nor drunkards, nor revilers, nor extortioners will inherit the kingdom of God."*

Looking at this in light of the understanding of the kingdom Jesus preached, is Paul speaking of where we go when we die or is he speaking of where God rules and reigns as King and LORD, and where His followers walk in true freedom? I believe it is the latter. It is sad to see a life controlled by the weakness of the flesh. They are not free to enjoy the blessings the LORD desires to bestow upon them, thus they are not a part of the kingdom Jesus preached. I know of many people that have had a salvation experience but are consumed by the lust of the flesh, or their own personal demons. They are not walking in what God desires for them. Will they spend eternity with God? That is a question only God can answer, but personally I believe they have missed the joy of their salvation, not their eternal destination. If we look at the lives addicted to alcohol or drugs, they are missing all the blessings and creating their own personal prison. God wants His children walking in freedom.

The kingdom of God is not a political movement. Some people have the mistaken idea that we can bring the kingdom of God in by political action. But it doesn't work that way. Though it is wise to vote our faith and convictions, and to make proper political decisions, the kingdom of God cannot be brought about this way. The kingdom of God is a spiritual reality.

We need to seek to find what God wants us to do, because what He wants to do, He will bless. The kingdom of God is where God is King. If God is our King, then we need to submit to and accept His dominion over our lives. Instead of deciding what we want to do and expecting God to bless it, we need to wait on His guidance. This is an important lesson we all need to learn. It is also more than just being under God's rule or His authority. Jesus' purpose in coming was to restore Relationship; the kingdom of God is about relationship.

Did Jesus bring in the kingdom? Jesus suggests in Matthew 11:12, *"from the days of John the Baptist until now."* Jewish understanding was that the forerunner of the Messiah would begin the process. Jesus was the one that brought forth the kingdom, but John started the process. So, did John bring in the kingdom of God? This is a tricky question and the answer is no. But John was instrumental in bringing the kingdom back.

THE BREAKER PASSAGE

The next Scripture we are going to look at was probably the most exciting passage for me when I first began my journey into the Jewish roots study. There have been some outstanding leaders in this movement, one of which was Rev. Robert L. Lindsey. He was a missionary to Jerusalem in the 1940's. He made many discoveries when he returned Scripture to its original Hebrew. He stated that "when we return many of the Greek passages back to Hebrew," we often get an "exciting light on what they really mean."[40]

This is truly one of those teachings and my favorite. It is found in Matthew 11 and is called the Breaker Passage. This is the most profound passage in our entire New Testament in its complexity. There are four or five messages in this one text alone that I could easily speak an hour on each. So, it will be necessary for us to just touch on the high points.

The account in Matthew tells us that while in prison, John the Baptizer sent two of his disciples to ask

---

[40] Robert L. Lindsey, *Jesus, Rabbi & Lord: The Hebrew Story of Jesus Behind Our Gospels* (New Orleans: Cornerstone Publishers, 1990), p. 61.

Jesus,

> "*Are you the Coming One or do we look for another?*" *Jesus answered...,"Go and tell John the things which you hear and see: The blind see and the lame walk; the lepers are cleansed and the deaf hear; the dead are raised up and the poor have the gospel preached to them.*" [Matt. 11:3-5]

Jesus did not answer them directly, but He quotes from Isaiah 61. He gave them the evidence of God's power breaking in. I believe what Jesus was saying was, "Who can bring in the kingdom of God except the King?" John's disciples then went back and reported that "**Yeshua** (Jesus) is the One, He is the coming King!" Jesus didn't look the way John expected; John expected judgment, but instead, Jesus came preaching peace, love, and the restoration of relationships.[41]

Jesus continued, "*Assuredly I say to you, among those born of women there has not risen one greater than John the Baptist, but he who is least in the kingdom of heaven is greater than he.*" [Matt. 11:11] Does that mean John was not part of the kingdom of God? The kingdom of God was one of the ways Jesus referred to His disciples, and John never became a disciple of Jesus. John was part of God's plan; he was one of God's chosen vessels from conception. John was the herald of the King, the one to make the way for the Messiah and he was prepared for that task before his birth.

So, when we become a follower of Jesus, we become a part of the kingdom of God. His Holy Spirit comes to dwell within us and with that comes His

---

[41] Phelps
, *Hidden Treasures Revealed, Part 1*, p. 95-96.

power. Jesus said, "*All authority (power) has been given to Me in heaven and on earth...and lo, I am with you.*" [Matt. 28:18-20] Jesus also proclaimed that His disciples "*shall receive power.*" ([Acts 1:8] Jesus was declaring that His followers would have His power, thus the least in Jesus' kingdom would have greater power than John.

I have been asked, "Did John not go to heaven?" Now this is a perfect example of the confusion about the term "heaven." Of course, John went to what we call heaven, but Jesus was not talking about John's eternal destination. Remember what the kingdom of heaven means: it's God's kingdom, God's movement for the here-and-now.

Jesus continued, "*the kingdom of God suffers violence, and the violent taken it by force.*" [Matt 11:12] The original Hebrew said, "**kingdom of God, violence.**" The translators had a choice either to understand this passage in a passive sense, "suffers violence," or in an active sense, "does something violently." The translators did not compare Jesus' words with Old Testament Scriptures, so they chose the passive position: "suffers violence." It should have read, "The Kingdom of God is breaking forth violently," instead of "suffering violence." Let's continue with Jesus' statement: "*and the violent take it by force.*" Jesus was saying that those that are a part of His kingdom are breaking out into freedom. Freedom from what? **Freedom from the control of the enemy and from the oppression of this world!** His followers are breaking out into absolute freedom in their lives.

Now let's look at the imagery that Jesus used here when He said, "*The Kingdom of God suffers violence, and the violent take it by force.*" He was actually quoting a

Jewish teaching based on Micah 2:12-13. In this imagery, God is saying, "I will gather my people in the corral and it will be noisy because of the multitude of people." Let me explain; a shepherd would stay out with his sheep at certain times of the year. The rest of the year he would take them out during the day and then bring them back in that evening. During lambing season, or when traveling long distances, he would stay out with his sheep overnight. Sheep are not the smartest animals, so they would wander off into danger. There were lots of wild animals seeking to devour the sheep, thus the shepherd would locate a cave or a bluff, or build a corral. He would find rocks and briery bushes to build up a wall around the sheep and then lay down at the weakest place, becoming the *"door to the sheepfold."* Recognize this phrase from John 10:7? In the morning, the sheep were ready to get out. They were hungry, thirsty and crowded.

Micah 2:13 goes on to say that *"The breaker is coming up before them."* Poretz is Hebrew for breaker. The *poretz* went to the weak spot and opens a hole in the wall. Jesus said of John the Baptist, "he is the *poretz*," the breaker who breaks a hole in the wall.[42] It goes on, *"They will break out, their King shall pass before them, with the* LORD *at their head."* [Mic. 2:12] The rabbis said of that passage, "The breaker will be Elijah and the one leading them out will be the LORD King, the King Messiah."[43] Jesus said *"and if you are willing to receive it, he* (John) *is the Elijah who is to come."* [Matt 11:14]

In Matthew 11:12, Jesus was saying that the kingdom of God is breaking out and those that are breaking out are breaking into freedom! He was not saying that the kingdom suffers violence or that it is violent. He was saying His followers will forcefully press into victory over the **oppressor**, against the enemy, Satan and his horde of demons. Jesus was saying His followers will seek after the kingdom of God with fervent zeal.

The beautiful thing about the sheepfold is that the minute the shepherd knocked the hole in the wall, every sheep makes the same decision, "I'm going to be the first one out!" They make a mad dash for the hole and knocked the wall down and get out into freedom faster and faster. That was Jesus' image for the Church! His followers would not only break into freedom, but they would also make the opening bigger so that others could gain freedom too. The Breaker Passage is critical to Jesus' understanding of the Church and His

---

[42] Bivin and Blizzard, *Understanding the Difficult Words*, p. 84-87.
[43] Lindsey, *Jesus, Rabbi & Lord*, p. 62.

kingdom. The kingdom of God is not passive; it is an active force in setting people free, and as they get free, they're setting others free, just like the sheep bursting out into freedom. Can you imagine how those sheep felt when the corral was knocked down and they went running out into freedom and the zeal that they experienced?

Malachi 4:2b, and 3a answers that. The problem is, once again, the translators made an error, just like with, "Kingdom suffers violence." Let's look at this passage. *"And you shall grow fat like stall-fed calves. You shall trample the wicked."* Do you see a problem with this translation? The Hebrew word *poosh* means to frolic, to leap, to bounce, to jump, but *poosh* was translated as "grow fat." I am not sure how this mistake happened, but modern translations, such as the NIV, have corrected this error. It states, *"And you shall go out and leap like calves released from the stall."* Do you know what the purpose is for the stall-fed calf? The calf is fattened in preparation for slaughter. God is saying you shall go out like those who were condemned and now you are being released into freedom.

I helped my father-in-law with his cattle. When they are pinned up for vaccinations, etc., it didn't matter the size, from the youngest calf to the oldest cow, you had better get out of the way when they were released. They kick up their heels and frolic. This is the imagery in this passage. Malachi 4:2a says, *"But to you who fear my name, the Son of Righteousness shall arise with healing in His wings!"* This is the passage the woman with the issue of blood trusted for her healing, and I imagine she felt like jumping for joy. She was free, after twelve years of bondage; she was free in every sense of the word! [Luke 8]

In the Matthew 11 passage, Jesus was saying, "Don't you understand? That pinned up condition is the bondage, and now I have come to set you free." I once saw a grown cow released that had been pinned up for a while. She came out with a bound and all four feet were off the ground, jumping for joy. Jesus expected that kind of exuberance and that kind of joy from His followers. Less you misunderstand, I am not referring to forms of worship. I am speaking about our lives, our daily walk with our Savior and LORD. We need to realize the joy that is ours; the joy in the victory over the darkness we were once in. If we're not experiencing that joy, then maybe we haven't fully understood the deliverance that God has for us.

Do we understand true freedom? We think of freedom as being able to do our own thing. Our nature is to resist having anyone tell us what we need to do. What would make us want to give up control and be part of His kingdom? When we realize how much God loves us and is looking out for our best interest, we have no problem trusting Him and submitting to His will. When we put ourselves under God's authority, He doesn't make us His slaves, He literally leads us into freedom.

Our ability to fellowship with God is directly related to our level of freedom. The more we remain bound by things within our lives, the more restricted we are in our walk with the LORD. The more freedom we gain, the greater our fellowship with Him can be. Can you see this? We choose what our relationship with God will be. Like the loving Father, He is waiting for our return with open arms, but **it is our move**.

The imagery that God uses here is His people bound up in their lives. The enemy's lie is that real freedom is what the world offers, but if we look closely, we can see the chains of bondage. It's the battle of the mind versus truth. Whose report are you going to believe? The world's report or the LORD's report? Jesus was telling us, "**If you want control of your life, you must give up control, and then God will return control to you.**" You must first be under His authority.

If the world could only see the opportunities that God has planned for them. Just like the word "salvation." When King Messiah knocks a hole in the wall, all those opportunities are available; they're bursting into freedom. It's the joy of kicking up their heels and experiencing life. Why? Because He came to *"set the captives free."* [Luke 4:18] *"Stand fast, therefore, in the liberty by which Christ has made us free and do not be entangled again with a yoke of bondage."* [Gal. 5:1] <u>When we submit to **His Lordship**, we are walking in true freedom</u>.

In August of 1985, I put my life under God's authority. I yielded to Him and let Him be King of my life. I began to experience true freedom for the first time. He gave me the right to make decisions and the power to walk it out! I am set free from the bondages of my life and I can choose not to sin. It was my nature to sin and sin controlled my decisions but I have been liberated and set free! This is Jesus' message to us and what His kingdom is all about!

CHAPTER THREE

SEARCHING

THE FIRST CENTURY

Before we look in depth at a major topic in Christianity, we need to understand some of the Jewish custom during the first century.

First, prayer shawls did not develop until the Middle Ages. Constantine, who had become Christian, tried to stamp out Judaism by making it illegal to celebrate the feasts, to worship on *Shabbat*, to read or possess Hebrew scriptures, or to wear fringes on garments. Thus, the Jewish people started wearing fringes on the inside of their clothing to keep God's Law and not be arrested. This garment was called a *tallit* which means "small covering."

We must always remember that the Jewish people are very much a part of End Time Prophesy. So, Satan has used willing vessels down through the ages to try to destroy them. Haman, Emperor Hadrian, Constantine, Hitler, and radical Muslims have tried to eliminate all Jews from the face of the earth and deny their claim to the Promise Land. Emperor Hadrian hated the Jews so much, he tried to erase Israel from history. He changed Israel's name to Palestine by Latinizing the name of their enemies, the Philistines.[44] Satan wants to make God's promises null and void by wiping out the Jewish people, but that will never happen because **God's promises are yes and amen!**

---

[44] Phelps, *Hidden Treasures Revealed, Part 1*, p. 7.

God commanded in the Book of Numbers that His people wear fringes on the four corners of their garments. In Jesus' time, the fringes were on the outer garment of clothing, the cloak, frequently referred to as the *m*ᵉ*iyl*, as opposed to the tunic which was the undergarment.[45] There is a lot of speculation as to what the outer garment looked like. It would have been made of one material which was part of the Kosher Laws known as the Laws of Separation. It may have been like a poncho, or a robe, with four corners, or a shawl thrown over the shoulder so that part of the fringes hung down the back or near the ground. There was no positive description of it.

In the scripture, we do have a detailed description of the fringes, *tzitziyot,* which is plural for *tzitzit* (fringe). Every Jewish person wore the fringes. Numbers 15:37-41 said that they were to wear a four-cornered garment with fringes on the corners. The four corners of the garment had a very significant meaning. In the prayer shawl of today, the corners are often referred to as the wings of the garment. If we look at Malachi, the last of the old Prophets, we will find a clue to their significance. The scripture said that God had cursed those who rejected Him and turned away from Him. In Malachi 4:2, God said, *"But for you who revere My name,"* or in other words, honor, treat with reverence, believe, trust, serve, and follow, *"the Sun of Righteousness will rise with healing in His wings."*

Now, that's an interesting statement because the word "Sun" is spelled S-U-N in English; the light of righteousness. It also says, *"in His wings"* not "in its

---

[45] Strong, *The Exhaustive Concordance*, p. 82; Hebrew word #4598.

wings." I know this because there is no "it" in ancient Hebrew. The word was either he or she, male or female. When the sages discussed this Scripture in depth, they decided that this Scripture was talking about a person. There question was, "Who is the person who is called, **'The Light of Righteousness'** who will rise with healing in His wings?" Their conclusion was that <u>it was the Messiah!</u> The word for wings in Hebrew is *kanaph*; that is the word we find in Malachi. But the word *kanaph* has an additional meaning: "corners."[46] When the New Testament translators translated from Hebrew into Greek, they didn't get a direct one on one correlation. So, when it was translated into English, they got, "the hem or the edge of the garment." (Remember, most New Testament scholars and Old Testament scholars didn't compare scriptures.) But the scripture is referring to the corners where the fringes are located. As we precede, hopefully you will see why this discussion is so important.

Second, the doctors of the first century knew more than we might assume. The Greek physicians of that day had done extensive study of the human body and had made numerous discoveries. The doctors in Israel were aware of the Greek medical understandings so they were capable physicians.

Third, in the first century, women gathered water daily. They went early every morning and/or late in the evening to the spring or to the well. It also was a time of socializing and a time of sharing what was going on in the community. By the way, the

---

[46] Strong, *The Exhaustive Concordance*, p. 65; Hebrew word #3671.

woman at the well in Samaria was there at noon time![47] Why would she be there at noon? She was an outcast, so she made sure that no one else would be there when she went. That's why when she encountered Jesus, she was shocked to see someone at the well at the hottest part of the day. We need to understand that women could not initiate divorce, so her husbands had either died or divorced her. But she was considered an outcast because the man she was living with was not her husband. She had accepted her status as an outcast, so she went to the well at noon. Understanding the customs gives us an insight into this account.

Fourth, biblical literacy was much higher in that time than it is today. Why? They heard scripture discussed, read, and preached on in the Synagogue. Scripture was taught in every home. The father was responsible for teaching the scriptures to his children. If the husband was a righteous man, he brought those teachings into the home and they were discussed. So, they heard God's Word in the home, in the Synagogue, and at the festivals. Additionally, boys began school at the age of 5 where they began memorizing the Torah.[48] Their skills of memorization were much higher than in the western world of today. They were not distracted by the things we are today. Their culture was different; they were focused on God. Everything in their lives, their *Shabbat* celebration and their festivals, was centered on being God's chosen people. This was the very heart of their lives and the very definition of their nation!

---

[47] Nelson *NKJV Spirit Filled Bible*, p. 1579, footnote 4:6.
[48] David Bivin, *New Light on the Difficult Words of Jesus: Insights from His Jewish Context* (Holland, MI: En-Gedi Resource Center, 2005), p. 4.

SALVATION

We have talked about the background, the culture, the way Jesus interpreted Scriptures, and how He taught. Now the question is what did He believe? The only way we can know what Jesus believed is by what He presented and what He taught.

I want to deal with Jesus' understanding of "salvation," because this is a term that we, in the Church, use all the time. The problem is that what it means to twenty-first century Christians is not what it meant to Jesus living in the first century! I want us to discover what He meant when He used the term "saved" or "salvation." Because of what we have been taught, the whole meaning of the word "salvation" is much more limited in its definition; its power has been stripped and even trivialized to an extent. I want us to search the scriptures for Jesus' understanding of salvation.

Let's start with the woman with the issue of blood. To understand this account and the ramifications of it, we need to know the customs, the laws, and the situation. We know that she had a continual issue of blood, which was most likely a menstrual cycle that did not stop. The account of this is found in three Gospels: Luke 8, Mark 5, and Matthew 9. They are parallel stories, similar, with slight variations in their accounts, which is expected from different eye witnesses. The woman's physical problem was very serious. Luke tells us she had been losing blood for twelve years and she had spent all her money on doctors, but they were not able to cure her problem.

Besides the physical problem, we need to

understand that as a Jewish woman, she was under rabbinical law. Leviticus 15:19-33 tells us that she came under the category of unclean. As an unclean woman, there were very specific requirements and prohibitions that were imposed. We assume the woman was married because it would have been extremely unusual for her to be single, and if she was a widow, it would have stated that. Under rabbinical law her sexual relationship with her husband had been put on hold. If the woman had children, the children were forbidden to sit or sleep where she had been. Virtually, all physical contact was cut off. Like those with leprosy, she would have been considered an outcast. In normal situations, the menstrual cycle was considered a temporary condition, but this woman's condition had gone on for twelve years, and her natural relations with her family would have been disrupted.

She couldn't carry out social activities of going to the market and purchasing food or collecting water because rabbinical law stated that if she touched anyone, she would make them unclean. She was cut off from her friends and from social interaction, but the worst thing was she couldn't go to the Temple. When one was declared unclean, they had to go through the *mikveh*, the baptismal pool, before they could go on the temple mount to be declared clean. Thus, she could not give a sacrifice for her sins, make a trespass offering, or worship God. She couldn't go to the Synagogue for weekly study of the Word or prayer. This was because it was considered an improper action for her to go out in public, to a social gathering, where she would have contact with other people. Her life was so far out of order. Every single area of her life, including her relationship with God, was disrupted.

Because the woman couldn't go out, she had probably spent hours meditating on the word of God and searching the scriptures for an answer for her healing. She found her answer in Malachi 3:20 in the Hebrew Bible. In the Christian Bible, it is Malachi 4:2, **"There is healing in His wings."** She knew if she could just touch the wings of Jesus, she would be made whole. We know she was seeking to touch the fringes because the scriptures say, *"There will be healing in His corners, or in the wings of His garment."* The scriptures tell of many that touched the edge of His garment and were healed. [Mark 6:56] The example of this woman is the only one that's been given to us in detail.

She heard that Jesus was coming to her community and I believe she thought, "If I can only touch the corner of His garment, I will be made whole." She made the decision to touch His wings. She knew it was risky for her to go out in public, but her life was at a point that she had to take desperate measures. If she went out in public and people recognized her, the priests could have had her stoned. But she believed that Jesus was the Messiah and decided it was worth the risk. She believed that she would be healed by Him if she could sneak through the crowd and touch His wings. And that was exactly what she did.

As Jesus walked through the crowd that had gathered to get a glimpse of this Miracle Worker, He was approached by a man named Jairus. Jairus, *Ya'ir'* in Hebrew, was the head of the local Synagogue. *Ya'ir'* said to Jesus, *"My little daughter lies at the point of death. Come and lay Your hands on her that she may be healed, and she will live."* [Mark 5:23] This is the account of the girl

Jesus raised from the dead. Jesus was on His way to Ya'ir's house when the woman with the issue of blood works her way through the crowd to Jesus.

I want us to visualize this; the streets, even in Jerusalem, were very narrow. Jesus had His entourage of disciples with Him, plus the people that came with Ya'ir. There was also quite a large crowd of people that were gathered waiting to see Jesus, as well as those that were following Him through the streets. The woman had to work her way through the crowd.

"Reach of Faith"

I'm sure she obscured her identity so she wouldn't be recognized. She then reached out and touched His fringes. Whether they were hanging down His back or close to the ground, we do not know. When she reached out and grabbed the fringes, a remarkable thing happens: **she was instantly healed!** Now, the law said that anyone she touched would become unclean. Instead of making Jesus unclean, He made her clean and healed! The power of God is greater than the law!

Immediately, Jesus knew someone had touched Him. It seems to us that she would have been shouting, "Praise God, I'm healed!" But instead, she slid back into the crowd and tried to hide. Jesus was a Rabbi and a strange man to her, and what she had done was considered improper in the society in which she lived. She had taken great risk by what she had done and she feared what His response might be. She tried to get away as quickly as possible.

Jesus asked, *"Who touched Me?"* His disciples answered, *"Master, the multitudes throng and press You."* The people were bumping into Him. He said, *"Someone touched Me, for I perceived power going out from Me."* [Luke 8:45-46] The woman knew she had been caught, so she revealed herself; she bowed down before Him, and submitted herself to His mercy. Jesus, instead of being angry, smiled and said, *"Daughter, your faith has made you well,"* or *"healed you,"* depending on the translation.

This is a perfect example of Jesus' understanding of salvation. The word *sozo* is commonly translated "to save, to be made whole" in Greek.[49] Jesus was saying that this woman had been made whole: "Daughter, **your faith has *saved* you**."

What happened to this woman? Everything has been restored to her. Everything! Her relationship with her family, she could go back to the Synagogue, she could go to the temple and offer sacrifices, and she could present herself to the priest to be declared clean! She was restored to God, her family, and friends. She was also restored to her responsibilities; everything was put back into order.

---

[49] Strong, *The Exhaustive Concordance*, p. 88; Greek word #4982.

HOW JESUS SAW SALVATION

How do most Christian think of salvation? The predominant thought of most Christians is in terms of going to heaven when they die. Jesus' understanding of salvation, which comes from the Hebrew word *yasha*, is <u>being set free, to be safe, restoration, deliver, victory in the here and now</u>.[50] Do you see a big difference here? Jesus' name in Hebrew is <u>Yeshua</u> which means salvation. The root word, to save, is *yasha*. *Yeshua* is the masculine form of the feminine word which was translated in the Old Testament as "salvation." *Yeshua* is actually short for *Yehoshu'a*, which is Joshua. Joshua in Hebrew means "The Lord is Salvation." When we see Je, Ja, Jo or Ye, Ya, or Yo in Hebrew, we need to recognize that this is part of God's holy name added to a person's name. *Ye* is 'the LORD' and *shua* is "salvation." *Yasha* literally means to be delivered from immediate danger.

Jews understood *yasha* to be referring to the present, to be delivered and living in freedom. If we are in relationship with the LORD now, we will be secure in the age to come. God's plan for His children is far more awesome than we have understood it to be. God wants His children not only accepting Jesus as their personal savior and have their sins forgiven, but He also wants them **walking in freedom and to have a living relationship with Him.**

Let me share an experience I had while living in Birmingham, Alabama. I was helping a ministry hold a yard sale to raise money for a mission trip to Mexico.

---

[50] Strong, *The Exhaustive Concordance*, p. 61; Hebrew word #3461.

Someone asked me about the prayer shawl and I was explaining the fringes and what they represented, the knots, and the colors. A lady overheard our conversation, came up to me and said, "I go to Temple Bethel (a conservative Synagogue), our Rabbi left some time back and we've been looking for a new Rabbi. We should have gotten you for our Rabbi." I thought to myself, "Lady, you really don't want me." I thought it was humorous, but I felt very complimented. As we were talking, her husband, who had been inside, came out red-faced and angry. He said, "I'll tell you the difference between Christianity and Judaism." Pointing his finger in my face he said, "Christianity is about death! Judaism is about life! Life!! Life!!!" Then he turned and walked away with his wife. As he left I realized that all he had ever heard about Christianity was about dying. Yes, we talk about Jesus dying on the cross, the execution stake, and that is essential. But all that Jewish man had ever heard was that Jesus died and when we die we're going to go to Heaven or Hell; it is all about what happens when we die, and Judaism is about living as God's people.

Hearing this wounded me because I knew he had never been told what Jesus said. *"I came that you may have **life** and have it more abundantly."* [John 10:10] Most evangelistic attempts are centered on "Where are you going to spend eternity? If you die tonight are you sure you will go to heaven?" All these statements are important, but they are predicated on dying. I truly believe the world really wants to hear "<u>what can fix my life!</u>" They are hurting right now, their lives are in turmoil, and their relationships are a mess. They want to know, "Can God help me now?" If all we focus on is the beyond, then we don't have an answer for this hurting world, for the here-and-now. Jesus' focus was on the now. The true concept of *yasha,* is to be set free; to have the hindrance and the obstacles removed.

The image God gave me of *yasha* was a narrow ravine that became narrower and narrower with two huge boulders on either side. Beyond the boulders there was a field with all the opportunities of life. I started moving toward the field and *boom,* I was stuck. People tried to help me, but there was no moving. Finally, I cried out, "God save me!" Two big hands came down and grabbed the boulders and pulled them apart. Then I was free to move into all the possibilities that God had created for me. *Yasha* means to have the hindrances, the obstacles, removed from our lives.

Now let's look at something that is mentioned three times in scripture. It is the "Finger of God." The first time is in the plagues of Egypt in Exodus 8:19. The second time was the writing on the tablets in Exodus 31:18 (the same account is also found in Deuteronomy 9:10.) And the third is in Luke 11:20: *"But if I cast out demons with the finger of God, surely the kingdom of God has come upon us."* In other words, salvation has to do with life being altered radically by the power of God. The way has been made broad for us to walk in total freedom and to pursue everything God has for us!

Jesus removed one of the major boulders, sin, between us and God, but there are more boulders than just sin in our lives. Some are there because we choose to put them there and some are there by nothing we have done ourselves. Sometimes boulders are there because the enemy has planted lies in our minds when we were very young and vulnerable. Because the lie has been there since childhood, the lie is accepted as a part of our makeup and thus it has become a huge boulder. One of the major lies the enemy plants in our minds is "I'm not loveable," and that is a lie from the pit of Hell because look at how much God loves you!

In the case of the woman with the issue of blood, Jesus was saying, "Daughter, your faith has allowed the bondage to be removed and you are now **set free and made whole.**" He put everything in her life back in order so that she could be what God created her to be from the very beginning: to walk with God, to have fellowship with Him, and to be in relationship with Him. So, the whole Bible is about God trying to restore that relationship that was broken in the garden.

WORK OUT OUR SALVATION

Paul wrote in Philippians 2:12, *"Work out your own salvation with fear and trembling."* That seems to be complete opposite of what Paul wrote just five years earlier to the Ephesians: *"not of works, lest anyone should boast."* [Ephesians 2:9] These two Scriptures, however, are not in contradiction. When we understand that salvation is not just about our eternal destiny, then Philippians 2:12 makes much more since. You see, God delivered us, but we must walk it out!

We need to be asking, "God, what part of me is still broken?" Can you say, "I am ready to accept what You want to do in me? I am ready to accept freedom and walk it out." That is God's desire for every human being on this earth, past, present, and future. Why else was Jesus' death required? **He paid it all!**

We must walk out our salvation day by day. The reality is, we make the decision every day: <u>do I obey God or do I choose to ignore His guidance</u>. Realize that it is a difficult thing to do. To successfully walk out our salvation, we must grow in faith and in the character of Jesus. In my reasoning, if God only wanted us saved so we could go to what we call heaven, the minute that we fell on our knees and received Him as Savior, He would take us to our eternal destination before we could mess it up. But He leaves us here and gives us responsibilities, tasks, and gifts to do His good will because it is the living of life that He is interested in, not just what happens when this life is at an end. God created this world and said, **"It is good."**[51]

Let's look at what can happen when we think we have gone far enough. *"And Terah took Abram and his grandson Lot…and they went out from Ur of the Chaldeans to go to the land of Canaan; and they came to Haran and dwelt there."* [Gen. 11:31] Now, where was Terah going? To the land of Canaan. Did he get there? No, he stopped in Haran, and he died there. He found a good place to settle; the fields were green and the neighbors were nice so Terah settled in. So what did Abram, later called Abraham, have to do? He had to finish the journey: *"Go out of your country, from your family and from your father's house, to a land I will show you."* [Gen. 12:1]

This is what happens so often in our walk with the LORD. We get enough relief that we are comfortable

---

[51] See Genesis 1:10, 12, 18, 21, 25, 31.

or we are satisfied with ourselves and our ministry. We may not realize it, but subconsciously we are saying, "God, this is as far as I want to go." But we have not yet reached the fullness God has for us. When we get relief from the bondage, we don't realize we are still confined. We must make the decision, **"I want all that God has for me."** God doesn't want us to just be content that our eternal destination is secure, He wants us free to be all He created us to be!

We all know John 3:16. "**Everlasting**" does not define the life, **it describes the life**. This scripture is telling us that the life God gives us is everlasting, which begins the day we are born into His kingdom, not the day we die. He wants us to decide to walk in that everlasting life now.

Once God was dealing with me. I said, "That's not me." Diann said, "Your problem is you just don't want to change." I said, "But, if I change, you might not love who I become." She said, "I will love you even more, because whatever God does in you will be even better." The enemy lies to us and causes us to fear the changes God wants to do in us. But we must be willing to **trust God** and to be ready to walk into all He has for us and into total freedom from the control of the enemy. God loves us so much that He wants nothing between you and Him but love! Nothing, not one sin, not one barrier, not one problem, He wants a total and complete relationship that is fulfilled by our daily walk, a daily expression of love and sharing. This is true salvation. This true relationship continues after we walk to the other side, where we see Him face to face.

Sometimes we get so disgusted with this world that we can't wait to get out of here, but even though it has been corrupted, it is still God's creation and we are expected to try to make it better. When we look at salvation as a promise that is going to come someday, we are missing the blessings that He intends for us right now. **Salvation is about being set free and walking in victory,** as God intended from the beginning. It is a promise for today, equipping us to live our lives daily in relationship with Him.

Let's look at Peter's sermon at Pentecost in Acts 2. Do you remember what happens after Peter finishes his magnificent sermon? *"The people are cut to the heart,"* and they cry out, *"Men and brethren, what shall we do?"* [Acts 2:37] What did they mean? "What must we do to be saved?" "How do we get free?" "How do we get deliverance from the bondage that we put ourselves in and which we live in?" Peter responded, *"Repent and be baptized, every one of you, in the name of Jesus Christ for the forgiveness of sin."* [Acts 2:38]

By the way, the word "repentance" does not mean to just say you're sorry. *Tesh'uvah* is the Hebrew word for repentance, literally meaning "return." The root word is *shuwb*.[52] Repentance is *metanoia* in Greek and it literally means "to turn around."[53] The word "repent" means not only to recognize the wrong, but to turn from it. We are told, *"If My people who are called by My name will humble themselves and pray and turn from their wicked ways, then I will hear from Heaven and will forgive their sin and heal their land."* [2nd Chr. 7:14] Turning from the sin is essential for one to be healed.

There are people that say that they have faith, but their lives never change. They do not understand

---

[52] Strong, *The Exhaustive Concordance*, p. 138; Hebrew word #7725.
[53] Ibid., p. 3341; Greek word #3341.

that they have missed it. Salvation is not just about getting saved and going to heaven. It's about turning our lives over to God. Having a life change is being made whole and seeking to walk in that wholeness. It's also about sharing this truth with others so that they can be brought into the kingdom. That is why God leaves us here and gives us His gifts: He expects us to build up the body so that the body can do the work that God has for us.

Peter also tells us, *"And you shall receive the gift."* [Acts 2:38] The gift that God gives is the Holy Ghost, the Holy Spirit, God's presence with us, and a restored relationship with Him. You see, the bride gets what the bridegroom has; it is common property. He takes what we have and we get what He has, and what He gives us is eternal life. See how much more the concept of salvation is than what it appears to be? If we comprehend that eternal life is given with the Holy Spirit for the here-and-now and it continues into eternity, what a message we have for the world!

ZACCHAEUS

I want to share the account found in Luke 19:1-10 of Zacchaeus who lived in a very prosperous town, Jericho. Zacchaeus, *Zakkai* in Hebrew, was a tax collector for the Romans. To be a tax collector, one had to submit a bid to the Romans on how much he would pay for the right to collect taxes for a particular area. If the bid was accepted, the tax collector paid Rome from what they collected. They taxed roads, bridges, produce, and live- stock at a high rate. Of the money that came in, the tax collector gave Rome the amount agreed upon and kept the rest for himself. It was a common practice for the tax collector to charge an enormous amount. The tax collectors were the most despised people because they were considered traders. They not only collaborated with the oppressors, but they lined their own pockets in the process.[54]

Zakkai was a chief tax collector, which meant he had other tax collectors under him of which he received a percentage of their profits. This made Zakkai a very wealthy man. In the KJV Bible we find tax collectors referred to as "publicans," meaning a public official. *"And behold, there was a man named Zacchaeus, which was the chief among the publicans and he was rich."* [Luke 19:2] They were so despised that they were considered their own set of sinners: *"a friend to sinners and publicans."* [Matt. 11:19]

Zakkai was hated by the people because of what he did, but what made it worse was what his name meant in Hebrew. Zakkai means innocent, so every time they called his name, they were calling out, "Hey, innocent one."[55] Talk about his name being bitter in their mouth! Remember, names in Hebrew are more than name tags; it spoke to the character of the person. But Zakkai was far from innocent.

"He sought to see who Jesus was, but he could not because of the crowd, for he was of short stature." [Luke 19:3] And you can understand why no one was willing to make room for him. *"So, he ran ahead and climbed up into a*

---

[54] Stern, *Jewish NT Commentary*, p. 30; Matt. 5:46.
[55] Ibid., p. 138; Luke 19:1.

sycamore tree to see Him, for He was going to pass that way." The tree the scripture is speaking of is a sycamore fig. It has low, sturdy branches, so *Zakkai* climbed up high enough to see Jesus over the crowd of people. It was important enough for him to make an effort to see Jesus. He didn't say, "Oh well, maybe another time." It was obviously important to him.

When Jesus walked by, He did a remarkable thing. He stopped and said, *"Zacchaeus, make haste and come down, for today I must stay at your house."* [Luke 19:5] In other words, Jesus was saying, "I want to go to your house and eat with you." In the Jewish culture, to break bread with someone is to enter into covenant with them. They did not eat with gentiles, publicans, or sinners, because that was accepting them as brother. The crowd couldn't believe what Jesus was doing. He had gone to be a guest with a man who was a sinner.

We don't know what happened inside *Zakkai's* house, but let's look at what he proclaimed to Jesus: *"Then Zacchaeus stood and said to the* LORD, *"Look* LORD, *I give half of my goods to the poor; and if I have taken anything from anyone by false accusation, I restore fourfold."* [Luke 19:8] Look at what he had just done. He had brought the severest penalty upon himself. You see, according to the law of that time, there were different levels of repayment. If a person confesses to fraud without malice, he was to repay that which was taken, plus twenty percent. The thief that is caught was to pay back double. But the person who maliciously takes what was needed for survival was to repay fourfold.[56]

What was Jesus' response to *Zakkai's*

---

[56] Ibid.; Luke 19:8.

proclamation? *"Today **salvation** has come to this house."* [Luke 19:9] Look at the man's life and what do you see? The proof of a totally transformed life.[57] Zakkai's life had totally changed. We not only see a change in his behavior, but also in his attitude, in his heart, and in his purpose. And Jesus called that salvation; <u>Jesus saw salvation as lives being put back in order.</u>

Is your life transformed? That is the only proof the world is going to believe. They don't want just words or another religion.; they want to see it in our lives, lived out in stressful situations.

I had the privilege of meeting Fred Bennet, who ministered to Jewish people. He shared an account with us of a Jewish man that broke my heart. The man's name was Chayim.[58] Chayim called Fred one evening and said, "Fred you'll never guess where I went last night." Fred said "No Chayim, where did you go?" Chayim said, "I went to a basketball game." Fred asked him, "Why did you go to a basketball game? You hate basketball." Chayim said, "Well, you see, these boys come to the Jewish Community Center where my brothers and I play cards. They tell us we are going to Hell if we don't accept Jesus. Well, their church league was playing last night." Fred cringed, because he used to referee, and he said he would rather referee an industrial league than a church league. That is quite an indictment, isn't it? Fred asked Chayim, "Why did you go to watch them play basketball?" Chayim replied, "I went to see if I could see Jesus. But I saw them yelling the same things that my brothers say, which they said

---

[57] Phelps, *Hidden Treasures Revealed, Part 1*, p. 38.
[58] Pronounced: Ḥayyīm or HYME.

we were going to hell for and I saw them throwing things at the referees. Fred, <u>I didn't see Jesus</u>."

Fred was heartbroken. He had worked with this man for years and in one night, these boys who proclaimed the name of Jesus, did not show the reality of Jesus in their lives. They felt secure in their eternal destination but had not allow the King of kings to change them and transform them into His image. People look at Christians and want to know, "Can I see Jesus?"

What Jesus brought is better than any reward when we die. He lives with us in the present. He brings us into the presence of the Living God who created us. He changes everything, if we will only let him.

THE LOVING FATHER

What is the parable that would tell us how precious we are to God? The Father that is willing to disgrace Himself for the sake of welcoming back His child that has gone astray. [Luke 15:20] You may ask, how did he disgrace himself? You see, everyone lived in villages for safety. They went out to their farms but lived in a community, so all his neighbors knew what his younger son had done. And, I am sure, they knew that he was returning and the shape the young man was in. They were probably expecting the father to reject him, but he didn't. Instead, he ran to greet him. In the first place, no respectable Jew of the first century would ever run; he walked with dignity. In the second place, no respectable Jew of the first century would bear his legs because he would have had to tuck his long robes in his girdle (sash), bearing his legs. But the father would do anything within his power to welcome his son back home.

"The Loving Father"

So, how did God disgrace Himself to welcome you and me back? Jesus hung on the cross, totally naked, carrying the weight of our sins. There is a weight to sin and He carried every sin that has been or ever will be committed. That is why it is so important to recognize that Jesus was sinless, else He could not have carried our sins for us.

Now, what three things happened when the prodigal returned home? The very first thing his father did was run to greet him, hug, and kiss him before anything was said. The Prodigal had planned to say, *"I'll be a hired servant,"* because a hired servant was a day laborer. [Luke 15:19] The landowner or foreman would go to the marketplace and ask, "Who wants to work for me today?" The landowner had no authority over the laborers except while they were on the job; they were not part of the household like the steward or the household servants were. See, the son was planning to be like a hired hand, or a day laborer, so his father wouldn't have any authority over his life. Now, when his father hugged and kissed him, he said, *"Father, I have sinned against heaven and in your sight, and I am no longer worthy to be called your son,"* [Luke 15:21] and he stopped. He didn't finish the statement. He saw the love of the father and his hard heart melted and he wanted to be restored. Do you see that <u>God's love is never ending</u>? The father didn't hunt him down and drag his son home; he gave sovereignty, free will, the right to make decision and mistakes.

  Here, the relationship is being restored! What was the next thing that the father did? He put a ring on his son's finger, a signet ring, which represented authority. This meant his signature was good, and he could make decisions for the whole family. What was the third thing his father did? He put his robe around his son, stating that everything he had belonged to the son. The boy had already wasted his inheritance, but it didn't matter. The father was saying, "I restore you to relationship, to authority and position, and to possessions. Now let's celebrate!"

  Incidentally, what is it that happens every time a sinner repents? *"There is joy in the presence of the angels of God over one sinner who repents."* [Luke 15:10] It doesn't say,

"The angels rejoice." So who is rejoicing? The LORD is the one rejoicing! What happened when Jesus sent out the seventy and they came back and said, *"Even the demons were subject to us in Your Name." **"Jesus rejoiced in the Spirit."** [Luke 10:21] That literally means He danced for joy; He rejoices when the kingdom goes forth and God rejoices in the presence of His angels! Now that preaches!

One Christmas eve, Ed Martt, Diann, another gentleman, and I went to the bars in Clinton, OK. I took my guitar and we asked permission to sing Christmas carols. They unplugged the juke box and even invited us back the next year. We ministered to a lot of hurting people that Christmas. When one lady was told, "Jesus loves you," she responded, "But you don't know what I have done." This is the lie the enemy whispers to us: "You have gone too far. God will never forgive you now." This is another lie from the pit of hell! There is no sin that God will not forgive. It is all covered under the blood of Jesus when we repent of our sins and receive His forgiveness. He welcomes us all with open arms and He forgives and forgets. The sin is wiped away and we are made new in God's sight.

So far, do you see how different this is from the way salvation is traditionally presented? If we could convey the sense of joy, the tremendous love, the wholeness, the message of what God wants for our lives, wow! But we must walk it out to tell it. We can't talk about the victory that Jesus brings if we don't have victory in our lives. That's why it's so important that we become mature enough that we can walk in victory. Then people will see it and ask, "How is it that you have so much peace? Everyone else is going crazy around you." You can say, "It's Jesus in my heart. It's the peace that He has given me." I read a story of a Christian man that worked in one of the top floors of the World Trade Center. He was often ridiculed for his faith and for having his Bible on his desk. When the planes struck the towers on September 11, 2001, they knew there was no way out. Because of his life, people came to him and he led many to the LORD that day. They knew he had a peace and a promise that they didn't have. Before those people went to meet Jesus that day, they called loved ones and told them about what this man had done for them.

There may be times when people ask, "How can you have such joy when your loved one has died?" The answer is, "Because I know what my loved one is experiencing and there's joy in my heart." See? In the midst of sorrow, there is joy. Joy is not dependent upon our circumstances, it is a gift from God and is dependent upon our relationship with the living God through His Spirit.

CHAPTER FOUR

FIRST CENTURY TOOLS

JESUS' SOURCES

We know Jesus spent hours before the LORD in prayer and meditated on the word of God. Remember all the times the Scripture tells us He went aside to pray.[59] Jesus was in constant communion with the Father, but He needed that alone time with Him as well. If Jesus needed alone time with the Father, what does that tell us about what we need? To truly be His effective servants, we must set aside quality time to be alone with our Father. I know, as a minister, it is too easy to count sermon preparation as our alone time, but God wants us coming to Him just to be with Him.

As for Jesus' sources, He quoted scripture all the time. When Jesus opened his mouth, we need to think Old Testament. Paul tells us, *"all Scripture is given by inspiration of God."* [2 Tim. 3:16] It is God breathed! So, what Scripture was Paul speaking of? He was referring to the only Scripture that existed during the first century: what we today call the Old Testament. Paul lived *"according to the strictest sect of their religion, a Pharisee."* [Acts 26:5] We might say he was an Orthodox Jew and he knew his scriptures. We must remember that the New Testament did not exist during Paul's lifetime.

There were also other sources that were used by

---

[59] Nelson's NKJ Bible, Matthew 14:29, 26:39; Mark 6:46, 14:32; Luke 6:12, 9:28.

Jesus and the New Testament writers. For example, there are a group of writings called the Apocrypha which the Protestant Church rejected but the Catholic Church included. Some of these writings have the appearance of being legend while others are very historical books, like the Maccabees. The reason that the reformers rejected the Apocrypha was because they did not meet the criterion that had been set up for Scripture, but they are historical and insightful in terms of the customs and practices. The books of what we call the Apocrypha were well known at the time of Jesus. John spoke of the celebration of *Hanukkah*: *"Now it was the Feast of Dedication in Jerusalem, and it was winter, and Jesus..."* [John 10:22] This shows us that Jesus was aware of the traditions that came from the books of Maccabees. *Hanukkah* is Hebrew for "dedication," and it celebrates the rededication of the temple after the desecration by Antiochus Epiphanies. This feast also celebrated the reestablishment of the independence of Israel under the Maccabees.[60]

Other writings that were used during the First Century were called Pseudepigrapha! "Pseudo" which means "false" referring to something that was written under a false name or attributed to someone that obviously did not write it. One example that is considered Pseudepigrapha is the Book of Enoch. It was developed during the inter-testimonial period and was a very influential writing. We find reference to the "Son of Man" in the book and it had tremendous influence on developing the idea of "Son of Man." It also helped

---

[60] Kevin Howard and Marvin Rosenthal, *The Feasts of the Lord* (Winter Garden, FL: Zion's Hope, 1996), p. 159.

shape the theology of some of the writers, such as Jude. Jude, and writings like his, did not explain their source because they expected the reader to be familiar with their sources, like the Book of Enoch; they felt it had spiritual validity!

Have you ever wondered why the Book of Jude talks about Michael the Archangel and Satan arguing over the body of Moses in the ninth chapter? It is found in the Assumption of Moses. This is a perfect example of a Pseudepigrapha writing. In the Assumption of Moses, there is a story about the Death Angel coming for the body of Moses, they argued, and Moses wouldn't go with him. The Death Angel went to the LORD and complained, "Moses won't go with me." God went to Moses and asked him, "Will you give up your life for Me," and Moses said, "Yes. For You I will." During Jesus' time, these stories were accepted as scripture and many of our New Testament books refer to some of those stories. When Jesus used the term "Son of Man," He was playing on the understanding that had been developed extensively through the Book of Enoch and other writings. The people of the first century had a profound understanding of what this term meant, which we are now rediscovering.

Other sources commonly used were the *Talmud* and the *Midrashim*. These consist of interpretive stories where scripture left unanswered questions, so it was their effort to fill in some of the blanks. This was where *Midrash Rabbah* came in. Sages sought to squeeze every drop of meaning from God's word. A good example of this would be the account of Miriam and Aaron's dissension against Moses and Miriam was struck by God with leprosy. [Num. 12:1-16] The sages looked at this event and said, "What is not being said here?" So, they looked at Numbers 12:1, *"Then Miriam and Aaron spoke against Moses because of the Ethiopian woman whom he had married."* Note, Miriam is named first. That indicates that she was the one instigating the action, otherwise Aaron would have been named first. The sages asked, "What was Miriam upset about to the point that she was questioning Moses and how he was the only one who could hear from God?" Their conclusion was that Moses had separated himself from his wife and was no longer sleeping with her, thus, Miriam was defending her sister-in-law, Zipporah.[61]

We find that *Midrash* was very influential on the New Testament, in the Gospels, as well as some of the Letters of Paul. *Midrash* was understood as being divinely inspired. We find that this technique was used in some of the New Testament writings. Does that make it invalid? No, because **God was in the process!**

Another source Jesus and the New Testament writers used was Aesop's Fables! Their principles were referred to and used in the rabbi's and Jesus' teachings. Aesop's Fables were widely known around the world at that time, and they were good moral, practical lessons. Jesus, like any good preacher, when He found a nugget, He used it! By understanding Aesop's Fables, we can gain insight into some of the scriptures.

We also need to understanding archeology and geography. Why did Jesus take His disciples to Philippi and Thessalonica? Where was it and why was the location important? Why was it so significant that Jesus grew up in the Galilee region and spent much of His

---

[61] Sifre Num. §99

ministry there? In seeking to understand Jesus and His ministry, it is important to understand the geography of the land. For example, when we realize that Nazareth was on the side of a mountain, we can understand why the angry mob was going to kill Jesus by throwing Him off a cliff. [Luke 4:29]

THE GOLDEN RULE

What we call the Golden Rule, "Do unto others as you would have them do unto you," was not original with Jesus. This is upsetting to some people because to them, Jesus had to be first to say all things. Why? If it is God's truth, **it's God's truth!** Whether it came from Jesus or it came from a great teacher, it is God's truth.

A personal note here: When I was a pastor in Oklahoma, one of my parishioners told me several times that she would hear almost the same sermon I had preached that Sunday morning on TV that same afternoon by a nationally known minister. Were we collaborating? Not with each other; it was the **Holy Spirit** giving the direction. It was a message God wanted His people to hear.

I want to interject a story here. Rabbi Hillel and Rabbi Shammai were visited by a pagan. He came to ridicule and trick them. He went to Rabbi Shammai, an ultra-conservative rabbi, first and said, "If you can teach me the whole of the law while standing on one foot, I'll become a follower." Shammai said, "Get out of here! There are too many Laws, there's no way. Leave!

That's ridiculing!" So, the pagan chuckled to himself and went to see Rabbi Hillel. He said to Hillel, "If you can teach me the whole of the law, while standing on one foot, I'll become a disciple." While standing on one foot, Hillel said, "That which is hurtful to you, do not do to others. The rest is commentary. Go study!"[62] You see, it is the Golden Rule, but in different terms.

That's the point: it's the Golden Rule! So, you see, although Jesus gave the positive side of it, when He said, *"And just as you want men to do to you, you also do to them likewise,"* [Luke 6:31] it is still a Pharisaic teaching. It was not unique or original to Jesus, but it is still just as important and valid!

Between the Old Testament and the New Testament, there were about 350 to 400 years. They were called the "Silent Years." Was God silent? No, God was still inspiring! His Spirit is still inspiring great teachers and interpreters today who study His word and seek to understand His truth. **God is never silent**. For us to think that during that 350-year period, God was silent and that no truths were being given is absolutely false! <u>When people study His word, God reveals His truth to those who seek Him.</u>

STYLE OF INTERPRETATION

The rabbis were most often members of the Pharisee party, or we might say denomination. They

---

[62] Stern, *Jewish NT Commentary*, p. 33; Matt. 7:12.

saw themselves as the spiritual descendants of the Prophets and they believed their responsibility was to interpret the scriptures for the purpose of helping the people know what God wanted them to do. The Pharisees stated that study was the highest form of worship. They emphasized that "<u>one studies to obey</u>." How can we obey if we don't know what God's word is saying to us or directing us to do? It is said that rabbis read the Scripture like blind men. How do blind men read? By feeling every bump and every wrinkle. We need to read our Scriptures like blind men, not just skimming through, but searching for the deeper meaning God has for us.

There were four methods of interpreting the text that the Rabbis used. The first method was *p'shat* which meant the simple or obvious meaning.[63] They always started with the simple meaning first. With *p'shat*, they took it for what it said in the text, with nothing added or nothing taken away. Once that was established, they would move to the more interpretive forms.

The second form was *remez*, which meant to hint or allude to, or to give a suggestion to. The text did not say directly, but hints to a scripture from the Bible (the Old Testament) or other known writings of the time. Jesus used *remez* all the time; this was His favorite method of teaching and explaining the Word of God. When Jesus taught, He did not quote the entire scripture, He only had to allude to the passage by pulling two or three key words out of a passage. Immediately, His listeners' thoughts went to the

---

[63] Stern, *Jewish NT Commentary*, p. 11.

passage and to the context of the passage. By saying just a few words, Jesus could take the crowd to the whole body of scripture in the Old Testament and bring that into what He was saying. They made the association and they understood what He was saying through allusion or even His actions.

For example, we made several references to *remez* earlier; Jesus used *remez* to identify Himself as the Messiah over and over again. Because He came in a culture that had certain expectations, He could not come right out and say He was the *Messiah*, so He used such terms as the "Son of Man," the "Green Tree," or the "Stone."[64]

When we read the New Testament, we need to keep one hand in the Old Testament because the Old Testament was the only Bible anyone had; it was Jesus' Bible. Let me give you an example of *remez* from the New Testament. If I say, *"For God so loved..."* did your mind go to John 3:16? That is *remez*; I didn't have to finish the Scripture because your mind automatically finished it.

Derash is the method of squeezing more meaning out of the Scripture.[65] The term *Midrash* came from *derash*. It is taking the Scripture, and like an orange peel, squeezing it to get every drop of juice from it; it's like taking every drop of meaning. We discussed this earlier in the story of Moses and Miriam.

---

[64] Phelps, *Hidden Treasures Revealed*, Part 1, p. 21, 39, 84-88, 91-98, 104.
[65] Stern, *Jewish NT Commentary*, p. 12.

Let me share an example of this from the teachings of the rabbis. Genesis 2:7 says, *"And formed man."* "formed" is spelled *yetzer* in  the LORD God The word inspirited; it is Hebrew. In this passage, the spelling of *yetzer* was incorrect. It was spelled *yyetzer*; it had two *yods*, which was a red flag for the rabbis. They felt nothing was in the Scripture by mistake, so they asked, "What was God saying?" Their conclusion was that when God created man, He inspirited him with two natures, *yetzer hatov* and *yetzer ha-ra*. *Yetzer hatov* is the inclination to do good and *yetzer ha-ra* is the inclination to do evil. They said the inclination to do good is to put God and others first, and the inclination to do evil is why a man builds a house, takes a wife, and gets a job.

You see, *yetzer ha-ra* in itself is not evil, in that it is the nature to provide for one's self.[66] Jews did not believe in original sin, instead they believed in the two natures of man. They said that the *yetzer ha-r* nature is so strong that if it is allowed to dominate, man will be led into sin. The law was God's way to help man keep the inclination to do evil in check, but we know that more is needed. We need *Yeshua*, Jesus in our lives to keep that inclination in check. Paul referred to this *midrash* in his teachings. [Rom. 7:13-25]

There are so many examples of d*erash* that I could share with you, but I will share some that have a direct effect on our New Testament writers. Exodus 32:16 reads, *"Now the tablets were the work of God, and the*

---

[66] Ibid., p. 370-371.

writing was the writing of God engraved on the tablets." When the rabbis read this, they stopped. This is the only time the word engraved, *kharut,* appears in scripture, which raised a red flag in their thinking. Yes, they knew their scriptures that well.

Remember, in ancient Hebrew there was no vowels and no punctuation. If the writer wanted to emphasize something, he would repeat it. Repetition was like an exclamation point. As for the issue of the missing vowels, the rabbis knew what the word was by the sentence they were reading, so they had k-h-r-t to work with. They questioned, "What if there was a hidden meaning in this passage? What if it was *kherut* instead of *kharut?*" When they saw that, they realized instead of it saying, "engraved on the tablets" it said, "liberty on the tablets." Just one vowel change made a world of difference. The law was not binding; it had set them free. We see this *midrash* referred to in James 1:25, *"he who looks into the perfect law of liberty."*

Matthew forms his own *derash* in Matthew 2:23,

"He came and dwelt in a city called Nazareth, that it might be fulfilled which was spoken by the prophets, 'He shall be called a Nazarene.'" First, the unusual thing in this Scripture is that Matthew did not name the prophet he was quoting. Second, it is not in the scriptures as such. He is taking Isaiah 11:1, "There shall come forth a rod from the stem of Jesse, and a branch shall grow out of his roots," and Jeremiah's references to the *"Branch of Righteousness,"* [Jer. 23:5, 33:15] and Zechariah's use of "branch." Zech. 3:8, 6:12] All of these scriptures from the writings of the Prophets refer to the "Coming One," the *Messiah*. Matthew took the word *netzer,* the word for "branch" which was written n-t-z-r and changed the vowels to make it *notzri,* which is "Nazarene."[67] He didn't change the text, he just changed the vowels. He was searching for the hidden meaning and that is what *derash* does. As far as Matthew knew, Jesus came from Bethlehem. For him, this *midrash* answered why Jesus went to Nazareth: to fulfill the Scriptures. I believe his interpretation came from the inspiration of the Holy Spirit.

    The last method of interpretation is *sod*, which is the hidden meaning, or allegory. This method is highly mystical and is seldom used in scripture, but it is used in the *Kabbala* and in *Gematria*. In the Hebrew alphabet, there are 22 letters. The letters are also their numbers. Their numbering system is: 1, 2, 3, 4, 5, 6, 7, 8, 9, 10, 20, 30, 40, 50, 60, 70, 80, 90, 100, 200, 300, 400. If two words have the same numerical value, the sages consider those two words linked together. For example, in the word for love, *ahavah,* the numerical value is 13. The

---

[67] Ibid., p. 14; Matt. 2:23.

word for unity, *Echad*, also has numerical value of 13. Love and unity are definitely linked, not only numerically, but in the definition of the nature of God. Perfect love and perfect unity add up to 26 which is God's holy name YHWH. This is an example of *sod*.

Another example is the prayer shawl where the word fringes, *tzitziyot*, is equal to 600, and there are 8 strands of cords and 5 knots. This adds up to 613, which happens to be the number of the Laws of Moses. This is why the fringes represent the law, so when a Jew wraps himself in the prayer shawl, he is wrapping himself in God's law. The Bible Code also uses *sod*. It can be enjoyable to play around with, but it can also be very dangerous.

CHAPTER FIVE

THE RELIGIOUS STRUCTURE

SECTS OF JUDAISM

We would call sects "denominations" in today's terms. There were twenty different sects during Jesus' day, including Pharisees, Sadducees, Scribes, Essenes, Zealots, and Herodias. The three main political and religious groups during the time of Jesus were the Pharisees, Sadducees, and the Essenes.

Pharisees, or *p'rushim,* which means "separated ones" in Hebrew, originated during the period of the Maccabees, from about 165 B.C.[68] They saw themselves as the decedents of the Prophets and they accepted the whole of the Bible. They were the rabbis and they believed in teaching and interpreting the law. They believed obedience was better than sacrifice, but they also believed that sacrifices were important. They forced the Sadducees to keep the ritual requirements of the Law concerning the Feast Days and they specified that it be done the way God had set it up in the scriptures. The Pharisees insisted that the letter of the law be kept. They were so concerned about people breaking the law that they developed the Oral Law or oral traditions. This law became so extreme that the common people felt they could not keep the whole of the law. This was why Jesus was so readily accepted by the common people. He showed them that God loved them, even when every letter of the Oral Law wasn't

---

[68] For more information, see www.wikipedia.com/maccabees.

kept.

Let me share an extreme example of the Oral Law. They expanded the commandment of Exodus 20:8, *"Remember the Sabbath and keep it holy."* They wanted to keep the people from breaking this commandment so, to clarify it, they made what is called "the fence" that consisted of 1,500 Laws on how to keep the Sabbath day.[69] It truly became overwhelming for the common folk.

Jesus was not a Pharisee Himself, but His methods and beliefs were more closely aligned with the Pharisaic. He was much more Pharisaical in His thinking than we are led to believe. Our Scriptures were written in a time when people knew that there were good Pharisees and bad Pharisees. Because of this, the writers of the New Testament assumed the reader would understand that they were not describing all Pharisees; they did not feel it was a necessary discussion.

Some of the different groups within the Pharisee party were first, the *Vathikin*, or the "strong ones," who rose at first dawn to pray. Second was the *Toble Shachrith*, or "morning baptists," who went through immersion before morning prayers; third was the *Kehala Kadisha*, or "holy congregation," who spent one third of their day in prayer, one third in study, and one third in labor. And fourth was the *Banaim*, or the "builders," who were into the mystical studies.[70]

I can tell you this: all Pharisees loved the LORD. The problem was that they were so hung up with the

---

[69] Cohen, *Everyman's Talmud*, p. 149-158.
[70] Alfred Edersheim, *Sketches of Jewish Life in the Days of Christ* (London: The Religious Tract Society, 1876), p. 224.

Word legalistically that they missed the revelation that came with it. Many could not see Jesus as the revelation because of their way of thinking. Thus, they missed the substance of the Word, which was and is *Yeshua*, Jesus.

We can do the same thing and miss God! When we get hung up with rules and regulations, we can miss His will, His direction, and His Spirit. I once heard Hal Lindsey's testimony. He said that when he got saved, he was on fire for the LORD, but he didn't know the rules. When church members started telling him he couldn't drink beer or cuss and be a Christian, he said he followed the rules but lost his joy. You see he wasn't, in his own words, "house broke." He went on to say God is much better at convicting His children of what they can or cannot do, but when God does it, we don't lose our joy.

I need to mention here that Synagogues were not houses of worship, they were *bet midrash*, a house of study. People would meet on the day of *Shabbat* and discuss, debate, and study the scriptures. To teach meant to explain scripture by scripture. So, to make a point, they had to have scripture to back it up. They would also meet there for prayers. The Synagogue became the center of the community and was the model for the first church.

As mentioned earlier, the Pharisees wanted the people to know the Word of God, so they set up schools in nearly every village in Israel.[71] The Synagogue was the school for the children. We sometimes have the misconception that Jews of the first century were uneducated and illiterate, but education was very

---

[71] Bivin, *New Light on the Difficult Words of Jesus*, p. 4.

important to them. One proverb said, "If you have acquired knowledge, what do you lack? If you lack knowledge, what have you acquired?"⁷² Memorization was a major part of their learning process. Sanhedrin 99a states, "If (the student) learns Torah and does not go over it again and again, he is like a man who sows without reaping."⁷³

© by Kreigh Collins 1948

The formal education for children began at the age of five. From age five, they were to study the Torah, the first five books of the Bible. At age ten, they studied the *Mishnah* (oral law), and by age fifteen, they studied the *Talmud* (commentary). ⁷⁴ If a student showed

---

⁷² Cohen, *Everyman's Talmud*, p. 173.
⁷³ Bivin, *New Light on the Difficult Words of Jesus*, p. 6.
⁷⁴ Samuel Safrai and M. Stern, *The Jewish People in the First Century:*

promise, he would continue his studies until he was seventeen. During that time, he would study and memorize the teachings of the prophets. If at seventeen he continued to impress the rabbis, he would begin his training to become a rabbi. I have often wondered if Jesus was one that continued His studies? We know He had to have shown promise since he impressed the rabbis when he was only twelve. [Luke 2:46-47]

The **Sadducees,** *Tz'dukim* in Hebrew, appeared on the scene at the same time as the Pharisees. They were the priestly line of Aaron, the Levites.[75] They were the Priest and the Temple officers. The High Priest was supposed to come from the descendants of Zadok, but this changed when the Maccabees took over around 165 BC.

The whole line of priestly succession started changing and by the time Herod was in charge, the High Priest had become a purchased position. Whoever had the money and was of the priestly line could become High Priest, therefore, the people in Jesus' day had very little respect for the High Priest. He was no longer seen as the voice of God, but a political figure. We could say Annas was the "godfather" of that day. He, as well as his five sons, served as High Priest.[76] In fact, it tells us in John 18:13, *"And they led Him away to Annas first, for he was the father-in-law of Caiaphas who was High Priest that year."* Why would they take Jesus to

---

Historical Geography, Political History, Social, Cultural and Religious Life and Institution (Assen: Van Gorcum, 1974), p. 953.

[75] Frederick J. Murphy, *Early Judaism: The Exile to the Time of Jesus* (Peabody, MA: Hendrickson Publishers, 2002), p. 237-241.

[76] Flavius Josephus, *Josephus, the Essential Writings: A Condensation of Jewish Antiquities and the Jewish War,* Translated and edited by Paul L. Maier, (Grand Rapids, MI: Kreger Publications, 1988), p. 280.

Annas first? He was seen by the temple guards as the one with the power.

The Sadducees did not believe in life after death, they did not accept the Oral Law, and it is hinted that they accepted only the first five books of the Bible, thus, they did not accept the teachings of the Prophets as inspired. [77] [Acts 23:8] We believe this because the Sadducees, in addition to the power of their position, lived off the sacrifices that were made at the temple. But what do the Prophets say about sacrifice? *"Though you offer Me burnt offerings...I will not accept them,"* and *"I have had enough of burnt offerings."* [Amos 4:22; Isa. 1:11] Over and over the prophets stated that obedience was better than sacrifice. It is easy then to see why the Sadducees would prefer the law over the teachings of the prophets. It is also easy to see why they didn't want to accept Jesus as the Messiah. His revelation at that time messed with their security, as well as their arrangement with Rome. Unlike any other conquered nation, Rome had given Israel the right to continue with temple worship and sacrifice. Thus, the Sadducees were politically driven to do whatever was necessary to protect their position.

Unlike the Sadducees, the **Essenes** believed in the immortality of the soul, and strived for purity and righteousness. They were basically of the priestly linage, but they disagreed with the temple leaders. They were also very pious in their beliefs. To join the Essenes, one had to turn over all their personal property to the community. They then had a trial period of three years before the property was

---

[77] Stern, *Jewish NT Commentary*, p. 18.

transferred to the group and became common property.[78] They did not marry, and it is believed that women were not allowed in the group. They preferred wilderness life, and were more isolationist. The Essenes were the ones that wrote the Dead Sea Scrolls and they called themselves the Sons of Light.[79] If you recall, Jesus refers to the Sons of Light in Luke 16:8. It is speculated that John the Baptizer was an Essene. They also believed in predestination: one was born a son of light or not. When Jesus said, *"you have heard it said, you shall love your neighbor and hate your enemies,"* [Matthew 5:43] He was quoting from the Essene teachings.

The **Zealots**, on the other hand, agreed with the Pharisees in their philosophy. They were what their name suggests: zealous to gain back control of their nation. They felt as God's people, He was to be their only ruler, and so they were the vigilantes of that day.[80] Rome was their enemy and they would do anything to take them out. They were known to carry knives under their garments, ready to strike back at Rome when the opportunity arose. There were some Zealots among Jesus' disciples, and I believe Judas was one of them. Some Zealots evolved into mere assassins called *Sicarii*.[81]

The **Scribes**, *saw-far'* in Hebrew, were extensively trained in the skills of reading and writing. They copied the Scriptures perfectly, and if they made a mistake, they had to start all over. They were in every

---

[78] Josephus, *Josephus, the Essential Writings*, p. 266.
[79] Flusser, *Judaism of the Second Temple Period*, p. xi-1;9
[80] Josephus, *Josephus, the Essential Writings*, p. 266.
[81] Henry Snyder Gehman and John D. Davis, *The New Westminster Dictionary of the Bible* (Westminster: Westminster Press, 1970), p. 1012.

Jewish party, and we know there were Scribes among the Essene community because of the Dead Sea Scrolls.[82] It took years to copy just one book of the Bible. I have seen an original manuscript of the book of Isaiah in a building in Israel dedicated to it, and it is unbelievably long. And to think a Scribe sat and wrote it all out is amazing.

Lastly, **Herodians** were the Jewish supporters of Herod and his actions. They were strong supporters of the Greco-Roman culture and were very liberal in their thinking. Furthermore, they despised the Essenes and the Zealots.

A DISCIPLE

We all know that Jesus had Disciples, but did you realize that it was a common practice for rabbis to have disciples? The word for disciples is *talmidim*. Do you recognize the word *Talmud* in *talmidim*? *Talmidim* literally means student; a disciple is a student. Some rabbis, like Hillel and Shammai, had academies. Disciples lived and studied at these academies, and these rabbis were stationary.[83] There were also itinerant rabbis that traveled and their disciples went with them. Jesus was an itinerant, meaning a traveling rabbi. Scripture tells us that someone said to Him,

---

[82] Murphy, *Early Judaism*, p. 215-216.
[83] Moseley, *Yeshua*, p. 156-157.

"'LORD, I will follow You wherever You go.' And Jesus said to him, 'Foxes have holes and birds of the air have nests, but the Son of Man has nowhere to lay His head.'" [Luke 9:57-58] Here Jesus was saying, "I don't have an academy or a house where I do My teaching, so if you want to be My disciples, you're going to have to walk after Me." In fact, when Jesus said, "Follow Me," those words in Hebrew literally mean, "Walk after Me. You walk where I walk. Walk with Me."

Now, there were certain expectations to be a disciple. A disciple was expected to memorize the teachings of his master. Jesus' disciples and followers walked considerable distances, and I am sure Jesus would have been teaching as they traveled. Whenever they heard Jesus teach, they had to memorize his words. To us that seems remarkable, but theirs was a life of devotion. It had been thought that writing down the words of the teacher wasn't allowed, but archeologists have discovered some written sayings of the rabbis, so that thinking had to be adjusted. When Jesus said, *"be My disciple,"* He was asking "are you willing to totally commit your life to Me?" Often, when we think disciple, we think follower, but we need to think student. The student made a life commitment to learn the words of his master because the teacher trained his disciple so that the disciple could repeat the teachings of his Master. The disciple taught in the name of his master. Here is an example of the way the disciples would teach: "Rabbi Yochanan said in the name of Rabbi Zinaim ..." In other words, "This is what my master taught me." The disciple would give credit to his master for the teaching.

That's why when Jesus said, *"You have heard that*

it was said, ...but I say," it was highly unusual. [Matt. 5:21, 22, 27, 28] He didn't follow the pattern and quote His teacher, but instead He took the authority on Himself! Therefore *"the people were astonished at His teachings, for He taught them as one having authority."* [Matt. 7:28-29] This meant that He was not depending on the authority of another and that was very unusual. Jesus was asked *"By what authority are You doing these things? And who gave You this authority?"* [Matthew 21:23] They were asking Jesus, "What Rabbi taught You to say these things? Who gave You the authority to be critical of the temple practices or of us? What are Your credentials? Who ordained You?" Jesus knew they were trying to trick Him, so He answered them, *"I also will ask you, ...the baptism of John-where was it from? From heaven or from man?"* [Matthew 21:25] In other words, "Did John learn through an academy? Did John's authority come from a rabbi, or did it come from God?" They were afraid to answer because the people believed that John was ordained by God, but Jesus didn't say God, did He? What did He say? "Heaven." "Did it come from heaven or from man," meaning God or man. Because the crowds were listening, those questioning Him were afraid, so they said, *"We do not know."* Jesus said to them, *"Neither will I tell you."* [Matthew 21:27] In other words, "If you're not going to answer Me, why should I answer you?" Jesus knew if He said, "I have been sent by God," they would judge Him and call Him a blasphemer.

Rabbis received their credentials by studying and going through an ordination process. Jesus' ordination was part of what His baptism was about because God is the one who ordains! Whether Baptist,

Presbyterian, Methodist, Catholic, Pentecostal, or any other denomination— they do not ordain. They hand out the ordination certificates and they have their standards, but God is the one who ordains; they only confirm what God is doing. That is sometimes forgotten; churches and denominations are not to ordain of their own authority, but to be God's vessels.

The Disciples memorized the teachings of their master, so that they accurately spoke in his name. So Jesus' disciples were expected to know the words of their Master and then go out and teach in His name because He was the authority! A disciple learned through three processes. First, through memorization, second by observing their Rabbi, and third by imitating their master. They observed their teacher to see how he responded to different situations or conflicts because they wanted to accurately represent him. Disciples were expected to act and speak like their master.

Therefore, if we're going to be disciples of Jesus, first, we're supposed to be students and **learn His teachings**. Then we're supposed to look at the life of Jesus and **observe His responses**, and last, we **imitate Him**. How do we know how to respond if we don't know what He said? We are to model our responses and our lifestyle after His! We are to walk in Him. What did Paul say about this? We *"are being transformed into the same image from glory to glory," "to the measure of the fullness of Christ...may grow up in all things into Him."* [2nd Cor. 3:18, Eph. 4:13-15] You see, the whole point was for His disciples, His children, to grow and mature in Him!

By the way, the word Disciple often refers to "son." Jesus said, *"If I cast out demons by Beelzebub, by whom do your sons cast them out?"* [Matt. 12:25] Disciples called their rabbi "father," so what did Elisha call Elijah? *"My father."* [2nd Kings 2:12] The disciples looked at their rabbi as father, for he was their teacher and they received their training from him. In fact, by tradition, they were told to pay more respect to their rabbi than to their earthly father because their earthly father gave them biological life, but their rabbi brought them into the "age to come," their eternal life.[84] If there was an issue between taking care of their earthly father or taking care of their rabbi, they were to give preference to their rabbi; this allowed them to walk away from some of their usual earthly obligations.

Paul said in 1st Corinthians 11:1, *"Imitate me just as I also imitate Christ."* Paul was taking on the traditional role as Rabbi to his students, or disciples, so he was saying, "if you imitate me, you imitate Christ, because I am trying to show you how He lived." That is the whole point. You don't just tell what the teacher said, you imitate that which gives authority to your words. The actions give validity to the teaching, and it confirms the truth of the Word! That's a message for all of us. That is why the Christian that says one thing and does something else is a hypocrite; their words are meaningless if they do not validate the Word with their lives, and the world will not listen. More damage is done by the one who proclaims the Word and lives the lie. William J. Toms said, "Be careful how you live, you may be the only Bible that some people ever read." The world is looking for proof, not another religion!

---

[84] Bivin, *New Light on the Difficult Words of Jesus*, p. 20.

CHAPTER SIX

DIFFICULT TEACHINGS

DEAD BURY THE DEAD

Sometimes Jesus' words seemed very harsh. Harsh enough to the point we might say, "I'm not comfortable with this passage." When we come upon these scriptures, the natural reaction is to just skip right over them. The next two subjects we will be dealing with will somewhat put us in that position. In them, it may seem Jesus reacted to the situation, but Jesus never reacted, He responded! **His response was always in obedience to the Father,** or else He would have sinned. Remember, every response, every word out of His mouth was in obedience to the Father. Or else, He was not the Messiah! Yes, that is a radical statement, but a true one. Because, if He had sinned, He could not bear our sins, for He would have had to pay for His own sins. Just one sin would have invalidated Him as the sacrifice for our sins. Remember Leviticus 6:6? The trespass sin offering must be <u>without spot or blemish</u>.

When we read our scriptures, especially the Gospels, and we find one of these difficult passages, we need to stop, pray, and begin digging. Usually one of these scriptures means there is a treasure to be discovered. There is something that we are not seeing, something that we are missing. I liken it to a buried treasure that we walk over and never know it is there, but when we begin digging and discover it, we are so much richer because we took the time to search.

We are going to explore an easily misunderstood text. One in which Jesus seems very harsh and uncaring. In fact, He almost seems cruel. If we are not careful, we can get a wrong impression from this text. Since we know this does not describe Jesus' nature, what is really going on here?

In this text found in Matthew and Luke, Jesus tells his disciples to *"depart to the other side. Then a certain scribe came and said to Him, 'Teacher I will follow You wherever You go.'"* Jesus responded, *"Foxes have holes and birds of the air have nests, but the Son of Man has nowhere to lay His head."* [Matt. 8:18-20] Jesus was telling the young man to count the cost. As we mentioned earlier, Jesus did not have an academy or a house, He was an itinerate Rabbi, a traveling Rabbi. He was not denying the scribe the opportunity to follow Him. Jesus just wanted him to recognize the cost of discipleship.

"Then He said to another, 'Follow Me'. But he said to Him, 'LORD, let me first go bury my father.'" [Luke 9:59] Matthew identifies this young man as a disciple, so he had been following Jesus as He went about Israel teaching. Jesus' response is where there appears to be a problem: *"Let the dead bury their own dead, but you go and preach the kingdom of God."* [Luke 9:59-60] On the surface it appears that Jesus is uncaring. Instead of giving the man who, it seems, has just lost his father sympathy and ministering to his needs, Jesus has harsh words. So, we must ask what was really being said here? What are we missing?

Things are not as they appear to be: there are some key issues in this text we need to figure out. In this passage, the man was not saying that his father has just died. Let me explain a Jewish custom of the first century that will help in the understanding of this text.

If the man's father had just died, he would not have been there speaking with Jesus, he would have been sitting *shivah*.[85] *Shivah* means seven days of sitting in mourning when there is the loss of a loved one. This tradition is based on the account of Joseph's mourning for his father, Jacob: *"they mourned there with a great and very solemn lamentation. He observed seven days of mourning for his father."* [Genesis 50:10] Joseph observed *shivah*, a week of mourning. Also in Genesis 7:4 in the account of Noah, *"for after seven more days I will cause it to rain."* I wonder if this was also a time of sitting *shivah* for his grandfather, Methuselah, or a time of mourning for what was to be.[86]

Sitting *shivah* developed into a very elaborate social custom. When they sit *shivah*, they wore clothes of a mourner, sit on the ground or low to the ground, and were not made comfortable by desirable food. They do not leave the home except for going to the tomb to call out the person's name during first three days. Do you remember where Mary was when Jesus came after Lazarus' death? *"Mary was sitting in the house."* [John 11:20] She was sitting *shiva*. There had been cases where people had revived up to three days after they were buried, so they would go to check if their loved one had revived. Does this explain why Jesus waited until the four days to go to Lazarus' home?[87] It was to show

---

[85] Moseley, *Yeshua*, p. 22, 180.
[86] When we add the age of Methuselah was when he begot Lamech, Genesis 5:25; the age Lamech was when he begot Noah, Genesis 5:28,29; the age Noah was when the floodwaters came, Genesis 7:6, it adds up to the age Methuselah was when he died, Genesis 5:27.
[87] Stern, *Jewish NT Commentary*, p. 165; John 11:19-20.

God's power, and to fulfill one of the four Messianic signs. The people knew that this was not a natural recitation, Lazarus was really dead, so it was a miracle to bring glory to God.

If the disciple's father had just died, he would have been home sitting *shivah*. So, either his father was near death, which is a possibility, or, more likely, his father had died almost a year before, and it was close to the time for the second burial.[88] Let me explain the second burial. After a year, the family would gather the bones and put them in an *ossuary*, a bone box, or in a family bone pile.[89] This was a social custom of that time. When he said, "Let me go bury my father," most likely the time was nearing when he needed to do his social responsibility. Jesus said, *"Let the dead bury the dead,"* or in other words, "The second burial is a social custom and God has a job for you to do **now**."

It is possible the young man's father had not died yet. His father may have been old or near death. In that case, the young man was saying that there were certain responsibilities of the world that he had to take care of before he could do what Jesus had called him to do. Matthew calls him a disciple, so he had already been following and learning at the feet of Jesus, and Luke takes it one step further: You go and preach the kingdom of God. He had been with Jesus long enough to be trusted with the message of the kingdom. Jesus was saying, "I have a job for you to do. There is a commissioning on your life. Go now and minister!" But this young man was finding excuses. How many down

---

[88] Moseley, *Yeshua*, p. 22-23.
[89] Phelps, *Hidden Treasures Revealed*, Part 1, p. 31.

through the ages have been called by God to serve and found excuses. Excuses like: when my parents are dead, when I am financially secure, when my children are grown, when I am old. It is never easy to let go and let God do what He desires in and through our lives. We are often afraid of being too different in the eyes of the world. There are always going to be things that hold us back from serving God.

If the young man's father was still alive, he was saying, "it will be easier to follow you after my father is dead." You see, in Jewish tradition, the son was expected to follow in his father's profession. If a son did not follow in his father's footsteps, he brought dishonor on the father and even on his own life. Jesus was saying, "if you follow Me, you have to walk away from things like security, home, family, and even the respect of others." The young man wanted to follow Jesus when it was comfortable and convenient, but <u>God's call on our lives is seldom comfortable or convenient</u>. You see, God had a job for this young man to do that was much more important than his earthly social responsibilities. Jesus' call was "you go" implying now, not tomorrow, or next week, or next year.

Now what did Jesus mean "Let the dead bury the dead?" Let those that are of this world handle the things of this world; those that are not a part of the kingdom of God are the ones to take care of the affairs of this world. Jesus was not endorsing irresponsibility. Instead, He was saying that these things cannot be our primary concern. Jesus said that our number one priority is God. And the young man had his priorities out of order.

Jesus wasn't saying, "don't be concerned for

your father," or, "don't take care of your father," or, "don't mourn." He was saying, "Put God first!" When you put God first, you will be amazed how everything else falls into place. He tells us,

> *"Therefore, I say to you, do not worry about your life, what you will eat or what you will drink; nor about your body, what you will put on. Is not life more than food and the body more than clothes? Look at the birds of the air, for they neither sow nor reap nor gather in barns; yet your Father feeds them. Are you not of more value than them? Which of you by worrying can add one cubit to his stature? So why do you worry about clothing? Consider the lilies of the field, how they grow; they neither toil nor spin; and yet I say to you that even Solomon in all his glory was not arrayed like one of these."* [Matt. 6:25-29]

When we are obedient and put God first, He will give us the strength, wisdom, knowledge, and skills to take care of all the other things that need to be done.

When we try to do these things on our own strength, we burnout. Burnout is when we exhaust our physical bodies, our emotional bodies, and our spiritual bodies. No one can do God's work on their own strength. It is not up to us to fill the church, or take care of every little detail. When we realize that the One who has called us and commissioned us will equip us, and when we put our priorities in order, God first, then we do not experience burnout. He gives us more energy, more time, and more ability, and we have more joy, more peace, and more fruitfulness because <u>we are not depending on our own strength</u>. When we put our lives, our family, and our ministry in His hands, we are putting Him first and allowing Him to be in charge, then our lives are in order.

Jesus was also saying, "Show Me more respect than you do your earthly father. I am your teacher." We find this thinking in rabbinical writing in the *Talmud*.[90]

CURSING THE FIG TREE

The next Scripture we'll tackle is a troublesome one. It begins in Mark 11:12. When we look at it on the surface, it poses a real problem for us because it appears that Jesus got angry, cursed the fig tree, and it died. Was anger ruling Jesus' actions? If so, that would be bad behavior.

This is a troubling scripture for us because it is out of character for Jesus. We must remember, Jesus never reacted to any situation, He responded! Reaction is an emotion; when something happens and emotions flair, we react. At that moment, our emotions are in charge of our lives and our actions. Jesus never did that. How do we know? He said, *"Whatever I speak, just as the Father has told Me, so I speak."* [John 12:50] Jesus only did what He saw His Father do, and only said what He heard His Father say. Had Jesus been ruled by His emotions, the Holy Spirit would not have been ruling in Him and He would have sinned. For Jesus to be sinless, every word from His mouth was for a purpose. To be

---

[90] Bivin, *New Light on the Difficult Words of Jesus*, p. 20.

sinless, He never had a hostile response or idle reaction to anything. Therefore, Jesus' actions were not a reaction, but a calculated response. There was a reason for Him doing what He did. So, when we run into a scripture that doesn't represent Jesus' true nature, we first need to pray and ask the LORD to reveal His truth to us. And then, like good detectives, we gather our tools and begin digging.

To understand the reason for this scripture and the message that is hidden in the curse, we need to understand the fig tree in Israel. If you remember the account of Nathanael's call to discipleship, he was sitting under the fig tree meditating on the word of God.[91] [John 1:43-51] The rabbis said the Word of God is like a fig tree. The figs ripen a little at a time and they cannot be gathered all at once, so it is with the Word of God. It must be read, re-read, studied, and meditated on repeatedly. The fig tree is a very important tree in the life of Israel and is a symbol for the nation of Israel and the study of the Word of God.

There are two facts about the fig tree that helps us understand what was happening in this scripture. Mark gave us some clues. The first clue we find is: *"seeing from afar a fig tree having leaves."* [Mark 11:13] This tells us that the leaves were mature because Jesus saw them from a distance. Mark also tells us in earlier passages that this occurred the day after the Triumphal Entry where Jesus entered Jerusalem at the beginning of the week of preparation for Passover. [Mark 11:9-12]

Since Passover takes place in our March or April, or, it would be in early spring. In the Jewish calendar,

---

[91] Phelps, *Hidden Treasures Revealed*, Part 1, p. 31.

they did not have 365 ¼ days like we do. Their calendar had fewer days, so they would add an extra month every so many years to bring the calendar back in line. They would add the second of Adar. Even when second Adar was added, the latest Passover could come would have been the last of our April. So, the account of the fig tree was in early spring. It is said that fig trees do not begin to leaf out until all chances of frost or freeze have passed. In fact, this is why Jesus said, *"Now learn this parable from the fig tree: When it's branches have already become tender and puts forth leaves, you know that summer is near."* [Matt. 24:32]

The second clue Mark gives us is, *"He found nothing but leaves, for it was not the season for fruit."* The fruit of the fig tree does not begin to ripen until, at theearliest, June. If it was not the season for figs, why would Jesus even go and look for fruit? To understand this, we come to the key that unlocks this entire passage for us: the fig trees in Israel begin producing fruit before they produce leaves. As summer draws near, the foliage comes on and covers the fruit. The leaves provide shade and protection for the fruit from the hot Israeli sun. Therefore, the sign of mature leaves is also the sign of mature fruit. <u>That's the key</u>! When Jesus saw that the tree had mature leaves, He knew it was giving a message that it had mature fruit, ready for eating. But the tree was guilty of false advertising. That is why when Jesus found no fruit, He spoke a curse over it.

"The Fig Tree"

There is one other thing we need to understand about this passage. Jesus had the anointing of the prophet. He spoke and acted prophetically. The prophet not only spoke, but he/she acted out the prophecy. This is what we call prophetic gesturing.

In the New Testament, we find an example of prophetic gesturing concerning Paul's future. *"A certain prophet named Agabus...took Paul's belt, bound his own hands and feet, and said 'Thus says the Holy Spirit, so shall the Jews in Jerusalem bind the man who owns this belt.'"* [Acts 21:10-11] Jesus used prophetic gesturing in His ministry. When the scribes and Pharisees brought the woman caught in adultery to Him, Jesus wrote in the dirt. [John 8:1-12] That was prophetic gesturing.[92] A major one was when Jesus overturned the tables in the Temple.[93] [Mark

---

[92] Phelps, *Hidden Treasures Revealed*, Part 1, p. 104.
[93] Ibid., p. 107-108.

11:15-17] We should never just skip over these hard passages. We need to stop, pray, study, and dig. We know Jesus' nature, He never let anger rule in His life. He did what He saw His Father do. He tells us, *"I and My Father are one,"* [John 10:30] so, what he did and said was what the Father would have Him do.

Do you see that prophetic gesturing was what Jesus was doing when He cursed the fig tree? He not only spoke God's judgment, but He produced God's judgment on the tree because of what the tree represented. The tree was lovely to look at, and it appeared to be mature. It looked so very fruitful but, in all actuality, it was barren. It was also taking all the nourishment and feeding for itself. The leaves are to bring nourishment in and to protect the fruit, then the fruit gives back its blessing. If we look at the tree as a person, it would be someone that seems so righteous and so good, but there is no fruit; there is no love, no joy, peace, patience, kindness, goodness, faithfulness, gentleness, or self-control. [Gal. 5:22-23] None of the fruit of the Spirit lives in them. The hypocrite puts on a false identity and pretends to be something he/she is not.

You see, that tree represents nations, churches, and individual lives in which hypocrisy rules. Jesus condemned hypocrisy more than anything else. This is one of the most destructive sins because it not only brings judgment on one's life, but it destroys the effectiveness of any kind of witness, as well as the Body as a whole. The world not only hears our words, they are looking for the proof in our lives. If it's not there, it does irreparable damage and destroys the effectiveness of the kingdom of God. Jesus told us, *"Whoever exalts himself will be humbled, and he who humbles himself will be exhausted."* [Matt. 23:12]

God expects His people to be fruitful, to bear the fruit of the Spirit. Why would Jesus say, *"let your light so shine before men, that they may see your good works and glorify you're the Father in heaven"* [Matt. 5:16] if our actions aren't important? When we let hypocrisy rule in our lives, we are denying the authority of the Holy Spirit and telling Jesus, "You are not LORD of my life." *"The LORD is near to those who have a broken heart, and saves such as have a contrite spirit."* [Psalm 34:18]

HYPROCRITES

Matthew 12, Mark 2 and Luke 6 all share the account of Jesus' disciples being condemned for breaking the law by working on *Shabbat,* Sabbath. The disciples were hungry, so they had gathered grain, and rubbed it in their hands and ate it. [Matt. 12:1, Luke 6:1] *"And the Pharisees said to Him, 'Look, why do they do what is not lawful on the Sabbath?'"* Jesus said to them, *"Sabbath was made for man, and not man for the Sabbath."* [Mark 2:24, 27] This was a Pharisaic teaching that existed before Jesus. The Sabbath was made after man was created, not mankind after the Sabbath, thus it was made for all people, to serve them. Jesus was saying, "Mankind is the Lord of the Sabbath. Do not let the Sabbath laws put you into bondage, it has been put there to be a help, not a hindrance."

That is why the attack of Jesus healing on the

Sabbath was so ridiculous. The Sabbath was a day designed to declare the holiness of God and to enjoy His holiness. What holier thing could Jesus have done then to deliver a woman who had been in bondage for 18 years, or to restore a man's withered hand? [Matt. 12:9-14; Luke 6:6-11] Jesus was putting things back in order and bringing back life! The religious leaders of that day had gotten so caught up in legalism that they omitted the Spirit of the law.

One thing we find Jesus attacking repeatedly was hypocrisy. Wherever He found it, whether from the Sadducees, Scribes, or the Pharisees, Jesus attacked it. The word hypocrite comes from the Greek word for actor. On the stage, the actor pretends to be something that he/she is not. In this context, it was not considered a negative term. Jesus used it as a negative term in life settings. He defined it as someone that said something one way and did another. Jesus was saying a person that does not present himself the way he is, is a hypocrite.

When Jesus said, *"Woe to you, Scribes, Pharisees, hypocrites,"* [Matt. 21:13] He was saying "Woe to you, Scribes, Pharisees, **who are** hypocrites." Do you see that "who are" is implied here? He was not condemning all Scribes and Pharisees; there were good Pharisees and Scribes, and bad ones. He was speaking of those that said one thing and did another. Many of the Pharisees followed Jesus' teachings. We know that Nicodemus was a Pharisee and became a follower of Jesus. [John 3:1-12] Also, Joseph of Arimathea who took *"the body, he wrapped it in a clean linen cloth, and laid it in a new tomb,"*

[Matt 27:57] was a member of the Sanhedrin.[94] He would have been either a Sadducee or a Pharisee, and I feel sure he was a Pharisee. There were many Pharisees that followed Jesus before and especially after His death.

He went on to say, *"You are like whitewashed tombs."* [Matt. 23:27] What did he mean by "whitewashed tombs?" To understand this, we need to look at the customs of the first century. It was very common for the dead to be placed in caves. The family that used a cave would whitewash the outside of it so it could be seen on a moonlit night. This defined the cave as a tomb, warning travelers that there were dead men's bones inside, since travelers would look for a place to stay at night and often use a cave for shelter. The whitewashing distinguished a tomb from a regular cave so that a traveler would not go into it and be defiled or defile the place of the dead.[95] Their understanding of being defiled was coming into contact with a dead body. An example of this would be in Jesus' parable of the Good Samaritan. The priest and the Levite passed by the injured Jew presuming that he was dead or near death because they would have been defiled and unable to fulfill their duties at the temple if they touched him. [Luke 10:31-32, Num. 19:14-16]

Concerning the whitewashed tombs, Jesus went on to say, *"which indeed appear beautiful outwardly, but inside are full of dead man's bones."* [Matt. 23:27] Jesus was saying, "You are not what you appear to be. You are a hypocrite." This was a sharp criticism to those in leadership that said one thing and did another.

---

[94] Stern, *Jewish NT Commentary*, p. 84; Matt. 27:57.
[95] See *The Complete Biblical Library New Testament Study Bible*, p. 505; Matthew 23:27.

CHAPTER SEVEN

THE HEART OF IT ALL

JESUS' HEART

When scripture is interpreted today, we can sometimes miss the meaning behind Jesus' words. We are now going to look at the central theme of all of Jesus' teachings. It is in a significant number of His parables, and is truly the reason for His coming.

This statement is going to sound radical but Jesus did not come to die on the cross! He did not come to be raised from the dead! Those were the means by which God accomplished His purpose. What Jesus came to do was to restore relationships. That is what we're going to find throughout this entire study. This is truly the most important thing to remember. **The reason for Jesus coming to Earth was to restore the relationship that had been lost.** In fact, if I could tell you in one word what the whole of the law is, that word would be "relationship." Everything God has done is about relationship, so Jesus' coming was all about relationship. Jesus defined everything in terms of relationship, whereas the Pharisees defined life in terms of strict obedience to God. Jesus' definition was not mere obedience, but the motivation behind obedience: **relationship**.

RESTORING BROKEN RELATIONSHIPS

Paul wrote that *"God who has reconciles us to Himself through Christ Jesus."* He continued *"that God was in Christ reconciling the world to Himself."* [2nd Cor. 5:18-19] The word he used for "reconcile" is a classical Greek word, *katallasso* that means to restore the broken relationship between a husband and a wife. It means to put back together a marriage that was intimate but had been destroyed and broken, and to restore it back to its wholeness.

In the book of Hosea, God gives us an example of that broken relationship with Him.

"Then the LORD said to me, "Go again, love a woman who is loved by a lover and committing adultery, just like the love of the LORD for the children of Israel, who look to other gods and love the raisin cakes of the pagans." [Hos. 3:1]

Israel was God's bride, but she worshiped other gods and ran after the ways of the world. What are the believers in Messiah called? The bride of Christ: *"He who has the bride is the bridegroom."* [John 3:29] Matthew, Mark, Luke and John tell us that *Yeshua*, Jesus is the Bridegroom.

We were created to walk in harmony and fellowship with God. In the garden, there was perfect harmony, perfect relationship, and full authority. Those things were all lost. The whole process of salvation is to bring us back to that relationship and make it possible again.

In the account of Zacchaeus, Jesus said, *"he also is a son of Abraham."* [Luke 19:1-10] Why did Jesus proclaim that? Because he hadn't been part of the family but he was restored because he wanted back in relationship with God, and the believing community. Jesus said, *"Today salvation has come to this house."* Salvation! Zacchaeus was restored in his relationship and Jesus calls that salvation. If we could only get that mindset. Man, what a message we would have for the world!

BORN FROM ABOVE

Let's look at the idea of being "Born again" from the Nicodemus account, which also translates as *"born from above."* [John 3:1-12] I believe what Jesus really said was "born from above," in other words "born of the Spirit." Nicodemus took it as "born again," as he responded, *"How can a man be born when he is old? Can he enter a second time into his mother's womb and be born?"* According to the Jewish understanding, there were seven ways to be "born again."[96] Nicodemus had been born again when he went through Bar Mitzvah, became an adult, repentance, was immersed, got married, became a rabbi and a teacher of rabbis. He had done everything that was available to him. The only two he had not gone through was to be crown king or when a person becomes a Jew who was not born a Jew, and Nicodemus was born a Jew.[97] So, Nicodemus was asking, "How could I be born again since I have been born again by all the ways available to me?" Jesus told

---

[96] Stern, *Jewish NT Commentary*, p. 165; John 3:2-3.
[97] Alfred Edersheim, *The Life and Times of Jesus the Messiah: Volume 1* (London: Longmans, Green & Co., 1896), p. 384.

him, "There must be a rebirth of who you are!" There comes a rebirth and with that there comes a new identity, a new person. Paul refers to that as being *"a new creature in Christ."* [2nd Cor. 5:17]

When does eternity begin? The very moment that we ask Jesus to forgive our sins, we are born again from above, and become part of His kingdom. The word "life" found in John 3:16 in Greek is *zoe*, which refers to the quality of life, combined with the word for "eternal." Eternal in Greek is *aionios,* which means everlasting. The Greeks thought of *aionios* was life without time or timelessness. The Bible always understands it as never-ending time. Since God is the only one eternal in time without end, what would eternal life suggest? God's quality of life for those who believe! When do we receive God's quality of life? At the moment we accept Him as our Lord and Savior, we enter His kingdom, and become part of His family.

Paul said, *"God, who has given us the Spirit as a guarantee."* [2nd Cor. 5:5] Here, he was saying that it is our down payment for the greater things that are yet to come. Does that mean that we must wait? No, because we have His Spirit right now! We will experience greater glory, but we have His presence and power right now. That is why Paul said, *"We are more than conquerors through Him who loved us."* [Rom. 8:37] He was saying that we are victors in Christ and there is nothing that God can't do, greater things than we could think or imagine.

Jesus is coming back for a church without spot, wrinkle or blemish. [Eph. 5:27] He is coming for an adult bride, not a child bride. It's the bride's job to prepare herself, "ourselves." The bride is brought to the groom, not the groom to the bride. In Genesis 24, Abraham sent his servant to get a bride for Isaac. The servant asks, *"What if she won't come? Do I take Isaac to her?"* Abraham answered, *"No. If she doesn't come, she's not the right bride."* The bride must come to the groom. We are **caught up** to Him, so when He comes and calls, we must be willing to go to Him. [1st Thess. 4:17] The whole concept is that He doesn't want a child bride. He wants an adult, mature bride. We are to grow in the Spirit, in our understanding, and mature in the LORD.

MORE PEACE, MORE JOY, MORE LOVE

The Bible that Jesus used was called the *Tanakh*, the Hebrew scripture. It was divided into three sections: the *Torah* is the first five Books, the Books of Moses; the *Nevi'im* is the Prophets; and the *Kethuvim* is the writings such as Psalms, Proverbs, Job, Esther, and the historical works like Kings, Chronicles, and Samuel. As we mentioned earlier, *"im"* is plural, hence the writings and the Prophets.

Of course, there was not a New Testament at the time, so the Word that Jesus lived His life by was the *Tanakh*. He was the living *Torah* Himself! Jesus' Bible was the Old Testament. The *Tanakh* is the foundation for our New Testament. We lose the richness of our scriptures when we separate ourselves from our foundation. Jesus' words cannot be fully understood without the Old Testament foundation!

I once told a Jewish man as much when he was challenging our tour group in Jerusalem. He said, "Your Jesus is a liar! Not only is He a liar but a despicable person, and He is not the Messiah!" God did not allow me to answer him, He shut my mouth, because the man had more to say. He was an Ascetic Jew, with the curls and the dark clothing. He continued, "Because in His name thousands have been killed!" He was red-faced angry! I answered him, "You're right. People have done terrible things in His name." I started naming off the Crusades, burning of Synagogues with people in them, the Pogrom of Russia, the night of the Tinkling Glass, and others. He was shocked at my response. I said, "It makes me look bad. It makes my faith look bad. It makes my Messiah look bad. And I can't call them brother! That is because the love of God was not in their hearts." He responded, "Well, He is not the Messiah!" I said, "Why do you say that?" He answered, "When the Messiah comes, there will be peace! There is no peace!" I replied, "Oh, but yes there is peace. It's not out there, it's in my heart. I have such love for you, and your people. And for this city and a love for this land, because of my Messiah!" God was giving me the words to say and it just flowed. Then I said, "You have to understand, everything that you are, I am built on." And I named Abraham, Moses, and the Prophets. When he left, he left with a big smile and said "Shalom," then I said, "Shalom," and we shook hands firmly. He held my hand for a moment, then he turned and went upstairs. I believe that man had a different view of Christianity and our Messiah from that day on and God did it, not me!

The message was that God had given me such

peace and such a love for His people and such a love for His Word! The message is that Jesus came to give us life. We need to show people what God has done for us. Paul said in Romans 11:11, we are *"to provoke them to jealousy."* We are to show that we have more peace, more joy, and more love then they do because of our Messiah. We want to make them think, "That's what I've wanted all my life!"

GOD'S PEACE

The quality of Jesus' character, found in Galatians 5:22, is listed in order on purpose, and they are in groups of threes. The first three concern our relationship with God, the next three are about our relationship with others, and the last three concern our relationship to life in general. They are built on each other, each depending on the others being in place, and in order. Let's look at them as building blocks; the foundational ones are love, joy, and peace. They are gifts from God, and they come out of your relationship with God. If we don't have love, joy, and peace in place, then we can't have the rest of them. Salvation reestablishes love in our hearts as our foundation. What did Jesus say about peace? *"My peace I give to you, not as the world gives. Let your heart not be troubled, neither let it be afraid."* [John 14:27] That means that in the midst of crisis, when it seems imposable to have peace, God's peace comes in and lifts us up.

In 2002, I preached the funeral of my five and half year-old granddaughter, Samantha. How could I do that? God's peace came in so unbelievably powerful, it was like a shot of energy and strength. Our whole family experienced this. She had died suddenly. We knew she was ill, but we didn't know what the problem was. Her parents took her to the hospital and the hospital did a procedure, but she didn't survive it. We were devastated. My son, Johnny, asked me to do the funeral, and then he said, "Oh no, that isn't fair." I told him to let me pray about it. Suddenly God's peace came in. I never realized the power in His peace until then. I had preached about it, I'd counseled on it, but I had no idea the power that was in His peace until I experienced it firsthand. It's a power that can lift you up above the situation and give you the strength to do what you have to do in the midst of sorrow. It is unbelievable to the world, they can't comprehend it. What did Paul tell us about this peace? *"The peace of God, which surpasses all understanding."* [Phil. 4:7]

With that peace came a joy! I found myself standing at the pulpit in the packed church; there were family members, minister friends, people from other cities, and people from the community that I didn't even know. I shared with them the joy we had with our granddaughter and the love that we had, and all the fun stories, the wildness, and the headaches that she had created for us, and all those wonderful things. Suddenly, I knew that there was no one in this world who could have done that funeral other than me and through His peace, God gave me the strength to do it. If we could walk in His peace, our lives would be made a lot easier and we could show the world what they are really hungry for.

When Jesus said "salvation," He was saying so much more than our eternal destination. It includes that, but let's look at what He gives us: His peace, His joy, His love, and His power. These are the awesome gifts God wants to share with us, to put our lives in order and allows us to start living the way God created us to live, for the here-and-now. To me, that's the victory, that's the Good News of the Gospel.

The Hebrew word for "good news" is *basar*. This Good News required the death of Jesus and the power of the resurrection, but God has won and that's why it is the Good News. That is what salvation is all about: living the Good News. A pastor friend of mine, Joe Brock, once said to me, "We're the seventh day people living in a six-day world." The seventh day is the day of rest. We're the people of God's rest but we're functioning in a six-day world where there is unrest. Our job is to bring that day of rest into a world that is hungry for it!

CHAPTER EIGHT

BACK TO THE KINGDOM

IN THE GARDEN

Where do we first find the kingdom of God? In the Garden of Eden! This is the perfect picture of what the kingdom of God is really all about. When we go back to the Garden, we find four basic truths.

<u>First</u>, the kingdom of God is characterized by a **relationship** between God and His creation, Adam and Eve. The Jewish understanding was that when they were first created, they were created as one being![98] God then removed from the man the feminine aspect to create woman. The word that is translated as rib is *tsela* or *tsal'ah*, which also means "side," like the sides of the ark or the sides of the boat.[99] Adam was created with both male and female characteristics, but God separated the feminine aspects from Adam to form Eve. That's why when man and woman come together in marriage, *"the two become one flesh"* [Eph. 5:31] again, in perfect unity. At least that was God's intent. Until the fall, Adam and Eve were not seen as separate, even though physically they were. After the fall, they were seen as separate because of the disharmony between them. We still suffer from that disharmony, even within our own bodies; we are at odds and fight wars within

---

[98] James Strong, *New Strong's Exhaustive Concordance* (Nashville: Thomas Nelson, 2003), p. 23; Hebrew word #1319.
[99] Strong, *The Exhaustive Concordance*, p. 121; Hebrew word #6763.

ourselves.

Marriage is so sacred to God because it is a reuniting of the original creation, one being, and one flesh! God made them into two and His plan was that the two would walk hand and hand as one. What happens when they become one? They become reproductive and fruitful. Unity produces fruit. That's the concept of creation. In the Garden, there was **perfect relationship, perfect harmony, and perfect unity**.

By the way, who was the relationship between? God, man, woman, and the Earth. The Earth, the animals, the trees, everything was involved in that relationship! There was perfect relationship, perfect fellowship.

God would come in the cool of the evening, and He would walk and talk with them. It was the most natural thing in the world because they were <u>created to walk with the supernatural</u>. They were the natural expression of God and they were created to recognize and enjoy the presence of the supernatural in their lives. God made Himself visible to them. Unlike Moses or any man, they could see God face to face because there was no sin in their lives. It was the natural order of things, primarily because of their innocence.

<u>Second</u>, they walked in **perfect obedience**. They did not question God, or doubt God, because there was no reason to. They totally trusted God. So how long did he live in the state of innocence? We don't know because the Bible doesn't say. Remember, the Bible compresses time. It goes straight from the creation of all things, including man in Genesis 1 and 2, to the fall of man/woman in Genesis 3. Maybe they walked in perfect obedience to God for years- we just don't know.

When do we start counting Adam's age, from the day of his creation or from the day he starts to die? The day he starts to die is the day that he sinned and was expelled from the Garden. There was no death or aging until man sinned. All we know is that they lived in that state as long as they trusted God and did not question Him.

<u>Third,</u> there was **perfect harmony**. They wanted what God wanted and they were in perfect harmony. This is where we see the multiple relationships of the garden. Right here, man was in perfect harmony with God; man and woman were in perfect harmony with each other, and with nature; nature was in perfect harmony with God, man, and woman. When that harmony was broken, every relationship was effected so that even the Earth was thrown into disorder, and we are still reaping the results of that.

Before the fall, the earth provided everything that was needed. They took care of the Garden and it provided for their need. Before the fall, we see that harmony is characteristic of being in perfect synchronization with the Spirit and the will of God. They wanted what God wanted.

What were the three temptations in the garden? <u>First,</u> *"the woman saw that the tree was good for food,"* <u>second,</u> *"that it was pleasant to the eyes,"* and <u>third,</u> *"a tree desirable to make one wise."* [Gen. 3:6] These three temptations line up perfectly with those listed in 1st John. <u>First,</u> *"the lust of the flesh,"* <u>second,</u> *"the lust of the eyes,"* and <u>third,</u> *"and the pride of life."* [1st John 2:16] If we look at them closely, these are the same three temptations Satan tried to tempt Jesus with. [Matt 4:1-11] All sins fall into these categories and lead to destruction.

A prophetic friend, N. H. Dutton, once told me that God told him, "for ministries/ministers to stand strong against the enemy, they have to keep their hands off the three G's: the girls/guys, the gold, and the glory." Do you see here the "lust of the flesh", the "lust of the eyes," and the "pride of life?" 1st John goes on to say, this *"is not of the Father but is of the world."* What happened after the fall? God told Adam that he was going to have to labor by the sweat of his brow and the earth will give him thorns and thistles. [Gen. 3:17-19] The harmony was gone!

There is one other element that I need to add to this. God's first command was to be fruitful and multiply. [Gen. 1:22] That's why the Jewish people understood that having a family is the number one responsibility after their relationship with God. God is always first and the relationship in marriage is second. Why? Because God's first command was to be fruitful and multiply. The first relationship that He created was marriage. Therefore, marriage was prized very highly in the Jewish community, and having children was a great blessing. A woman who was unable to have children was considered cursed by God!

The fourth Kingdom principle is **positional authority.** What is positional authority? Mankind was given authority over the Earth. What was God's second command? Subdue the earth and take dominion over it. [Gen. 1:28] To subdue the earth means to establish one's self as having authority over it. The Earth is not just going to produce; one must establish authority over it. The Scripture tell us in Hebrews 2:7, *"You have made man a little lower than the angels... have set him over the works of*

Your hands…put all things in subjection under his feet." Why would God say to this creation He just made, *"subdue it; have dominion over?"* God told man and woman to take dominion *"over every living thing,"* every creature, *"on the Earth."* [Gen. 1:28] Man was created in God's image, and while he was under God's authority, he had dominion over every living thing and the Earth itself, because of his position. **God only gives His authority to those who are in a relationship with Him.**

That is part of what Jesus brought back: He brought back authority! The authority was given to the first Adam. The last Adam, *Yeshua* Jesus, had the right to that authority because He did not sin. As a result, He was given all authority, and He gave it to all of His followers. His authority is present today!

I want to share some of my personal experiences on this topic with you. While walking early in the morning, I've had dogs challenge me, and I said, "In the name of Jesus, you will not harm me!" I've had them stop barking, stand perfectly still, and just watch me walk away or start walking with me. When I spoke the name of Jesus with authority, without fear, and with the understanding that I am supposed to have authority over the creatures of the Earth, I've not had the first problem with a single animal. One Doberman even jumped the fence and ran toward me. When I spoke in Jesus' name, he stopped in his tracks, watched me for a while, and trotted back to the fence. God is good, all the time!

What kind of authority am I talking about? <u>The authority of the steward that takes care of his master's property</u>, and all of his master's business, doing so in his master's best interest. The steward knows that it is not his property, but that he is responsible for it. Understand this, the key to stewardship is that the steward treats the master's property the way the master would treat it himself. That's what stewardship means in scripture. The steward was responsible and faithful to the nature and the character of the master in using it, doing it in the master's best interest and ultimately in his own best interest as well. Christians should be the best environmentalists in this world, in proper balance. God has given us a great responsibility. We not only benefit from what the earth provides, but we need to be good stewards and care for it as well because it's our Father's world.

Do you remember the parable of the three servants who were given stewardship in Matthew 25:14-30? One was given five talents, one was given two talents, and one was given one talent. The man that was given five went out, invested it, and made five more. The man with two also doubled his master's money. The man with one said, *"I knew you to be a hard man..., and I'm afraid, and... I hid your talent in the ground."* What was the master's condemnation? *"You wicked, slothful servant! You knew"* what kind of a man I was and you did not act accordingly! He wasn't punished because of what he did, he was punished because of what he did not do. He did not act according to the roll of the steward, which is to deal with the property the way the master would have done it!

Now, if we have been entrusted with the mystery of the Gospel, we're supposed to be dealing with the Gospel the way the Master Himself would. We have been entrusted with the Earth, and we're supposed to be dealing with the Earth exactly the way the Master Himself would be doing it. We are to be God's representative. That is what I mean by positional authority: we have authority only if we are in proper position. We could also call it relational authority, because of our position in the relationship. That is why we have the right to use Jesus' name with authority.

Understand that in Middle Eastern cultures, a name is more than an ID tag; the name equals the character, the very essence of the one named. A perfect example is found at Rachel's death: *"And so it was, as her soul was departing* (for she died), *that she called his name Ben-Oni; but his father called him Benjamin."* [Gen. 35:18] In Hebrew, *Ben-Oni* means "Son of my Sorrow," whereas *Benjamin* means "Son of my Right Hand."[100]

So, to bestow a name is to exercise authority over it by giving it its character. That's why Jesus would tell the demons to be silent and not use His name when they called out– they were trying to exercise authority over Him by gaining power through the name.

Fellowship and relationship was necessary for Adam to fulfill his role of positional authority. There is a Jewish teaching on this I think that it's beautiful. It's based on the account of when God brought the animals to Adam to name. [Gen 2:19-20] When God brought the animals for Adam to name, He was saying, "Adam, I'm giving you a role to play in this creation. Now you stamp them with their character, their identity and their nature." That was the Jewish understanding of this passage. The Talmud tells a story about a master-painter. Every stroke of the brush was carefully placed and every color was carefully mixed and chosen.

---

[100] See Nelson *NKJV Spirit Filled Bible*, p.57; Genesis 35:18.

When he was finishing a magnificent masterpiece, he called his young son over and put the brush in his hand. Down in the right-hand corner he left a blank space, totally empty. He said to his son, "Finish the painting. I want you to be a partner in this." The sages said that this was exactly what God did with Adam. God was saying, "I made this wonderful creation but there is a little corner unfinished. I want you to finish the work, I want you to name the animals." God gave Adam the right to be a partner in creation, the opportunity to be with God in this whole process and share in the beauty that He made. He let His young son join Him in making this beautiful masterpiece. You see, that's the kind of relationship God shared with Adam in the Garden.

And that is the kind of relationship God wants with His children, to give us dominion, but we must want it. We must see ourselves in that kind of intimate relationship with the Creator of the Universe.

WHERE ARE YOU

What happened when the fall came? Everything was lost! Look at all the things that were totally destroyed with the fall.

What was the first experience of the Man and the Woman as soon as they ate of the fruit? They had shame in front of each other. That perfect harmony, that perfect fellowship between them was broken. Suddenly they realized they were naked, and they covered themselves with leaves. There was no shame before sin entered the picture.

What happens when God came looking for Adam? Adam, *"Where are you?"* [Gen. 3:9] This is an interesting word, "where." There are different words for "where" in the Hebrew language; this particular word can sometimes be called locative. For example: Where did I put my keys? What location? The way it is used here is more of a rhetorical question. For example, if you invite a couple to your house for dinner, and only one shows up, you might ask, "Where is your husband/wife?" You really don't want to know the location, you want to know why he/she isn't there.

When God said to Adam, "Where are you?" He was asking, "Why aren't you where you were? Why is your relationship different?" Remember, God knew from the beginning what Adam would do and He knew what was going to happen. **Nothing surprises God**. If He knows the number of hairs on our head [Matt. 10:30], He knows what we will do before we do it.

The question, "Where are you?" had to do with relationships. Again, the first thing that was broken was relationship. When man was told, *"You can be like God,"* Satan was saying, "You don't have to be under God's authority anymore. You can make your own decisions." [Gen. 3:5] That is why Adam's sin was disobedient. What happened the minute the fall came? Everything fell apart, all relationships were broken, and disobedience and rebellion became the norm. The harmony was destroyed between man and woman; between man, woman, and the Earth; and between God, and man and woman.

Who is called the god of this world after the fall?

Satan! Who was intended to rule the world? Man! God gave man the authority as long as he was under God's authority. Mankind was not created to stand alone, he was created to live under authority. By sinning, he put himself under the authority of Satan and the result was that he became part of the kingdom of darkness and fell from the kingdom of God.

According to Jewish understanding, the Garden of Eden was taken up into the heavens.[101] That's why they see Paradise as meaning "to be taken into the spiritual realm," not into heaven as we think of it. That is why the Jews felt that the righteous went into the Garden, back into that perfect relationship, that perfect harmony. They believed the Garden was taken up so that man would not try to get to the Tree of Life.[102] By the way, who is the Tree of Life? We understand it to be *Yeshua*, Jesus.

Everything was lost after the fall. Man can make his own decisions because he has free will, but he can no longer make ruling decisions; he no longer has the authority over the world. Now, he must force the earth to yield. He must suffer at the hands of a disruptive world. The results of the disharmony with the earth are: floods, droughts, famine, diseases, earthquakes, tornados, hurricanes, and all kind of problems. These things did not exist until the fall. Every part of creation was put into disharmony, and mankind and Earth began to die the day sin entered the world.

Jesus came to put creation, mankind, and everything back into the relationship that God had

---

[101] Cohen, *Everyman's Talmud*, p. 385.
[102] Ibid., p. 388.

originally designed it to be in. So, Jesus took us back to the Garden as our starting point, from which we are to mature and grow into that relationship. The only way that relationship can be restored is for the disobedience to be reversed. If disobedience meant death, *"The day that you eat of it you shall surly die,"* [Gen. 2:17] then death had to be paid for. Jesus paid the debt we could not pay and He brought those that would follow Him back to the relationship of the Garden. As the old hymn, *In the Garden* expresses God's heart, "And He walks with me, and He talks with me." <u>This is truly the relationship God desires with all His children. He desires to talk to us more than we want to hear from Him.</u>

MAN'S RULE

Mankind does not rule the Earth as a monarch, but as stewards, which means we only have the right to rule if we are under the Master's authority. And who is the Master? **Father God is the Master**, and it is His authority to give. That's the key! This is what I call positional authority; for man to be able to make decisions, certain things must be in place.

<u>First</u>, we must have the ability to make decisions about what is right and what is wrong. To do so, we must have freedom of will and choice; to be held accountable, we must be able to make decisions. In the situation where someone else makes the decision, the response is often, "Don't blame me if it fails!" Does that sound familiar? Does that sound like Adam? God

asked, "Have you eaten from the tree," and Adam replied, "It's not my fault." Who does he blame? Not Eve, but God! *"The woman You gave me."* [Gen. 3:12] In other words, "It's Your fault because if You hadn't given me that woman or made her that way, it wouldn't have happened." To have free will, we must make decisions and then we are responsible for those decisions.

The <u>second</u> thing we must have is authority. In scripture, authority is the right to rule. The Centurion came to Jesus and said, *"LORD, my servant is lying at home paralyzed."* Jesus replied, *"I will come and heal him."* The Centurion said, *"I am not worthy that You should come under my roof. But only speak a word and my servant will be healed. For I also am a man under authority... I say to one, 'Go,' and he goes; and to another, 'Come,' and he comes."* [Matt. 8:5-13] The Centurion understood authority and he recognized that Jesus was under God's authority, thus if Jesus spoke it, it would happen. Jesus replied, *"I have not seen this kind of faith in all of Israel!"* To have authority, one must be under authority, and God is the supreme authority. That's why Jesus did not operate under His own authority but submitted Himself to the Father's authority. Thus, Jesus was perfectly obedient, operating in the world under the Father's authority. What Adam should have done, Jesus did.

Speaking of God's authority, did you ever wonder why the women going to Jesus' tomb ask, *"Who's going to roll away the stone?"* [Mark 16:3] Jesus' tomb was for a rich man, so most likely the stone sat in a track with a stone wheel about 3 to 4 feet tall, and three or four inches thick. The tomb entrances were very low, and three or four women could have rolled the stone back and opened the tomb. Their question was not because the stone was so heavy, but who had the authority to break the Governor's seal so they could get into the tomb without getting arrested. That was the real issue: who had the authority to break the seal. The tomb had been sealed by Pilate with a wax seal, the stamp of the Roman Governor's seal. Whoever broke it would have violated Roman law and could be put to death. So the question was, "Who will roll back the stone? Who has the authority?" And when they got there, they found that God had said, "I have power over all rulers, I will break the seal Myself!" Who does Revelation tell us is worthy to open the seal? *"Who is worthy to ... loose its seals? Do not weep. Behold, the Lion of the tribe of Judah, the Root of David, has prevailed to open... the seals!"* [Rev. 5:2] **Yes, *Yeshua*, Jesus**!

The <u>third</u> thing that we need in order to exercise authority is power. Power gives the ability to carry out authority. For Man to exercise authority over the Earth, he must have all three: <u>the ability to make decisions, the right to make decisions, and the power to carry it out</u>. These are all foundational understandings that undergirds the whole concept of the **kingdom of God**.

KINDS OF POWER

There are three basic kinds of power in this world. The <u>first</u> is concrete force. This is where <u>physical force</u> is used to make something happen. This is best described as brute force! The second type of power is assumed power. Where there is a need for leadership, someone steps in and assumes and exercises power, and others let them. It can be good or not so good. Let's say there is a church, and no one will do anything unless Uncle Joe says it is okay. Uncle Joe has no position on a board, but he is the one that exercises power, and no one wants to face the consequences of opposing him.

These two forms are not God's way of taking authority. God does not want man to rule by brute force or assumed power. The only genuine power, the third type is delegated or assigned power. This is the kind of power that is granted by the order of a superior. The Jewish people understood that the authority came to them from Moses. Moses selected the 70 judges who became the forerunners of the great Sanhedrin of Ezra's and Jesus' day. They not only had the right to make decisions, they also had the power to carry those decisions out. They could have people beaten, thrown into prison, or fined. They established this power through their lineage from Moses.

In reality, there is only one power that exist in the world and that is the power granted by the Creator, God Almighty, the Supreme One. With positional authority, God gives us the ability to make decisions and the authority to carry out those decisions. His power is there to back it up when we are in line with His will and under His leadership. That is why we call it positional or relational authority.

Do we have power over the weather, such as tornadoes? Yes, we do when we are operating under God's authority. What about over animals? Yes, we do.

How about situations? Yes, we do. This authority is not for our own convenience; this authority is granted by God to those in communion with Him. We must be in such harmony with God that when we speak, we are speaking with God's blessing. That is the key! But there can be no fear or doubt, because when fear and doubt come in, we are allowing Satan to rule, not God. We must walk in the assurance that God is God and we are His. *"I can do all things through Christ who strengthens me!"* [Phil. 4:13] The power of God is there to serve the will of God, not the whims of man.

In 1988, God made His authority very evident to our whole family. We traveled with a pop-up camper from our home in Clinton, OK to Pensacola, FL for our last vacation before our daughter, Kim, went off to college. After driving for 23 hours, we arrived at Biloxi, MS in the middle of tropical storm Beryl. It was raining so hard we couldn't see five feet in front of us. Then our 1979 Dodge van flooded out in the middle of town; it had happened before so we knew it was the distributor cap, and we realized the danger we were in. Our thirteen-year-old son, Johnny, asked, "Dad, have you prayed?" The answer was no, so my wife and I laid hands on the dash and took authority over the van, and then I tried it again. It started right up. To say the least, we praised the Lord!

We arrived at Santa Rosa beach and set up our camper, but tropical storm Beryl was sitting right on top of us. It finally stopped raining Sunday morning, but instead of heading to the beach, we went to church. As soon as we returned, it started raining again. I had had enough. I told my wife, Diann, that if it didn't stop by morning, we were heading home. Our daughter,

Kim, was sound sleep but she sat up and said, "Maybe we are praying the wrong prayer." We had been pleading with God to stop the rain, so instead we began praying, "God send the rain where it is needed." The next morning, we woke to birds singing and no rain. I turned on the TV and the weatherman said that the most unusual thing happened, tropical storm Beryl back tracked (X) miles and went up the Mississippi River to the drought stricken areas of Tennessee and Kentucky. (I believe that was the states he mentioned) God was showing us His power and authority.

The most dramatic demonstration was yet to come. The last day I headed out early to fish. I went out on a sand bar that had been formed by the storm. I cast out my line and caught a skip-jack right away. The strange thing was that the skip-jack was swimming toward me. I then saw him in the wave with a shark chasing him. I kept reeling the skip-jack in, even though my reel was acting like it had sand in it. Then the skip-jack swam past me into the pool between me and the shore with the shark in hot pursuit. They went into the shadows and I realized that I was in danger. I spoke, **"In Jesus Name,"** with authority, and the shark immediately broke off the chase and went out to sea. I reeled the skip-jack in with ease to find the hook trailing behind him. I set him free and praised the LORD for what He had done. During that entire trip, God was teaching our whole family what positional authority was. And what an awesome learning experience it was.

CHAPTER NINE

GOD'S PLAN

RECONCILED

We find in Paul's second letter to the Corinthians an extremely important passage: *"If anyone is in Christ, he is a new creation."*[2ndCor.5:17] Do you see the connection to creation here? *"Old things have passed away. Behold, all things have become new,"* again! *"Now all things are of God, who has reconciled us to Himself through Jesus Christ, and has given us the ministry of reconciliation. That is, that God was in Christ, reconciling the world to Himself."* Then he said, *"Committing to us the word of reconciliation." "Now then, we are ambassadors for Christ, as though God were pleading through us: we implore you on Christ's behalf, be reconciled to God."* [2nd Cor. 5:17-20] This scripture says it so well!

Do you see how many times Paul used a form of it the word "reconcile?" To reconcile a relationship, the relationship has to be broken before it can be put back together again. Paul was saying that in Christ, God is restoring the relationship that was broken in the garden. As we mentioned earlier, reconcile in classical Greek is *katallasso*, which refers to restoring the intimate relationship between a husband and wife.

The Greek word *ginosko* means "to know," indicating empirical knowledge: to know a thing because it was studied or observed, to know someone's name. Whereas the Hebrew understanding of the word *yodah* is to know because of experience, knowing by sharing life, a relationship with the known.[103] *"Adam knew his wife and she conceived and bore a son."* [Gen. 4:1]

The LORD said that to me when I was trying to figure out the Holy Spirit. He spoke to me and said, "John, you are asking the wrong question." He then asked me, "How do you know your wife? Do you analyze her? Or do you experience her?" At that time, we had been married 21 years and there was no way I could analyze her, but I knew her because we had shared life. The Greek understanding of "to know" is to analyze, but the Hebrew understanding of "to know" is to experience!

In the *Septuagint* (translated Scripture from Hebrew to Greek) they used *ginosko* because it was the word that was closest to *yodah*. The New Testament translators did the same thing when they used the form *ginosko* implying "a be aware of."[104] That's important because we are told to know God and to know Christ, but it is more than knowing about, more than head knowledge. It is about being in relationship with the known, it is up close and personal! "To know" was an expression of relationship, and we are told to know Him! **God wants to restore the intimate relationship of shared life, of fellowship, with His children that was destroyed in the Garden.**

In the passage found in Matthew 7:21-23, as well as in Luke, Jesus said, *"Not everyone who says to Me, 'Lord! Lord!' shall enter the kingdom of heaven."* What did they say to Him? "We did this in Your name, we did that in Your name," Jesus said, *"I never knew you."* In

---

[103] See *The Complete Biblical Library, Old Testament Study Bible*; Gen. 4:1.
[104] Strong, *The Exhaustive Concordance*, p. 19; Greek word #1097.

other words, "We never had a relationship. You knew about Me, you knew My name, but we never had a relationship." That says volumes, doesn't it? He goes on to say, *"Depart from Me, you who practice lawlessness,"* or *"doers of iniquity,"* meaning lawbreakers. He uses this term because they were acting in Jesus' name without His authority to do so. Doing good deeds is not sufficient, He requires a relationship with the doer!

So, the <u>first</u> thing that was broken in the garden was **relationship** and the <u>second</u> thing that was broken was **obedience.** Obedience is doing what we are told to do, right? *"Without faith, it is impossible to please God."* [Heb. 11:6] How does faith and obedience fit together? This is one of my favorite coin principles. Faith is one side of the coin and faithfulness is the other. The word *emunah* means **faith** and it also means **faithfulness**.[105] Back to the coin principle, we can't have one side of a coin without the other. If we only believe, what does James tell us? *"Even the devils believe and tremble."* [James 2:19] <u>Faithfulness is demonstrating faith through our actions,</u> in other words being obedient to the Father. Coming into the kingdom of God means **embracing God as our LORD!**

Why is that important? Do you remember the birth announcement of Jesus? There were three titles given to the shepherds: *"Born to you this day in the city of David a Savior, who is Christ the Lord!"* [Luke 2:11] "**Savior**" <u>speaks of His path as the one who brings redemption</u>. "**Christ**," <u>Messiah in Hebrew, speaks to His anointing</u>. "**LORD**" <u>speaks of His authority</u>. **He is Christ the LORD.** God's kingdom is not a democracy; it is an absolute

---

[105] Stern, *Jewish NT Commentary*, p. 538; Gal. 2:16.

monarchy! If we're not willing to obey the King, then how can we be a part of the kingdom? The kingdom of God is made up exclusively of the people who choose to follow and obey King Messiah.

Disobedience is rebellion, so the only way to live in the kingdom of God is to walk in obedience. Jesus was perfectly obedient in His life; He demonstrated the way we are to walk in God's will. Remember the word *sh'ma*? <u>Sh'ma means to listen, to understand, and to obey</u>. *"Obedience is better than sacrifice"* is proclaimed in 1 Samuel and repeatedly in Deuteronomy. The Greek equivalent to *sh'ma* is *akouo*, which also means to listen, understand, and obey. God expects obedience. Jesus said, *"If you love Me, keep My commandments."* [John 13:15] "You will" is implied. So, "If you love Me **you will** keep My commandments," or, "You will be under My authority and you will be faithful to Me."

If Jesus came to reestablish relationship, He had to bring obedience back as well. I know that's a sticky point for most of us because we don't like the word "obey," or anyone telling us what to do, but this is a matter of choosing life. If we choose to disobey God, we're putting ourselves under Satan's authority. Do you remember the song from the Sixties, "Gotta Serve Somebody?" It said, "Well, it may be the devil or it may be the LORD, but you're gonna have to serve somebody."[106] Satan's lie has always been that you can run your own life, but if you're not serving God, guess who you are serving? Jesus said, *"No servant can serve two masters."* [Luke 16:13] He didn't say there was a third

---

[106] Bob Dylan, "Gotta Serve Somebody," recorded 1979, track 1 on *Slow Train Coming*, Columbia.

option. I can't say this enough: we cannot walk in disobedience and be a part of the kingdom of God!

The third thing lost in the garden was **harmony.** Jesus came to restore harmony. The Hebrew word for harmony is s*halom. Shalom* has more than one meaning; we know it means "peace," but it also means relationships in right order, a sense of well-being and it has overtones of good health and prosperity in the since of anything he put his hand to prospers and succeeds. What is Jesus called in Scripture? ***Sar-Shalom***, the Prince of Peace!107 [Isa. 9:6]

Jesus came to reestablish peace and to restore harmony between God and man! Harmony with God must be reestablished first, then harmony within ourselves can be restored. Only then can *shalom* between mankind be reestablished, and we can truly *"love thy neighbor."* [Matt. 19:19] Jesus came to reestablish the harmony that was broken in the Garden, a harmony within ourselves. When Jesus taught the kingdom of God, He was talking about bringing back the relationship, the harmony, the ability to walk and talk with God.

Harmony is wanting what God wants and being in perfect sync with the Spirit of the LORD. Paul said, *"If we live in the Spirit, let us also walk in the Spirit."* [Gal. 5:25] The word "walk" used here suggests a military march, an army in perfect step, and the one calling the cadence is the Holy Spirit. I've seen some crack drill teams and the leader doesn't even have to say anything. He turns and everyone turns right with him because they're so in tune with each other. Paul was saying that when God

---

107 Stern, *Jewish NT Commentary*, p. 106; Luke 1:79.

moves, we are to move right with Him, walking in perfect harmony, sensing God's will, God's way, and not missing a step. Jesus came to bring mankind the opportunity to walk in that perfect harmony with God.

The <u>fourth</u> thing that was broken was **positional authority**. Jesus came to put us back in proper position. He desires to restore us to the authority that was given to us in the very beginning. This is the authority to act as God's ambassador or representative so that we can do God's will on Earth. Exercising power without authority is rebellion. In Matthew 7:23 Jesus was saying, "You had no relationship with Me." God's authority is only given to those that are in a relationship with Him! Those that act in Jesus' name without authority are breakers of the Law! God's law says that when He gives us authority, the power will be there to back us up. But if we are not under His authority, we do not have the right to exercise that authority. A perfect example of that is found in Acts 19:13-16. The seven sons of Sceva saw the miracles and the deliverance Paul did and they decided that they could do that too. So, they spoke to the demons, *"We exorcise you by the Jesus whom Paul preaches."* There is power in the name of Jesus, but look what happened. The demons said, *"Jesus we know, and Paul we know about, but who are you?"* In other words, "You do not have the authority to use the name of Jesus, so we do not have to be subject to you!" The man possessed by the demons began to beat the men and chase them away. To use the name of Jesus with power requires a personal relationship with Jesus. His power and presence must dwell within you! Jesus' name is not a magic word.

When we call on the name of Jesus, we are

calling on the One who owns the name. We are calling on the person, the power, and the authority, not the word. To use the name of Jesus with power requires a personal relationship with *Yeshua,* Jesus. What Jesus said in Luke 9:1 shows that He had both authority and power. He gave authority to the twelve when He sent them out in His name to take dominion over sickness and demons.

Upon the return of the seventy, He rejoiced. He said, *"I saw Satan fall like lightning from heaven. Behold, I give you the authority…over all the power of the enemy."* [Luke 10:18-19] That indicates that the enemy has certain authority and power. Jesus was basically saying, "I give you the right to use My name and the power of God will be there to back it up." When we act in obedience, we will see the power of God in action. The key is that we must be willing to submit to the Father, and that's hard for most of us to accept. We don't like submitting to authority, but we must! <u>The only way we can have authority is to be under authority</u>.

THE LORD'S PRAYER

Jesus' model prayer to His disciples, found in Matthew 6:9-12 and Luke 11:2-4, amplifies what we should seek for our relationship with God. It states, *"Hallowed be Your Name,"* in other words, "the LORD's name be sanctified!" It goes on to say, *"Your kingdom come, Your will be done."* He was saying "May Your kingdom become more of a reality in my life than it has ever been!" Basically, He was asking His disciples and us to be willing to pray: "God, take authority over my life! Rule in me. Let me be a subject, one of your citizens. Help me to be obedient to Your will." Does this change how you look at this prayer?

When we read, *"On earth as it is in heaven,"* we automatically think of our eternal destination, don't we? This is another example of a bad translation. It should read, "On earth and in the heavens." If we could think for a moment of heaven as being more than just a place, and realize it is the supernatural realm beyond this world, Jesus was saying, "Your will be done in the spiritual dimension as well as on this earth." In other words, "May God's will be done everywhere and over everything."

When we are doing God's will, we have a dramatic effect on the powers of darkness. Paul tells us in Ephesians 3:10, *"The manifold wisdom of God might be made known by the church to the principalities and powers in the heavenly places."* In Ephesians 6:12, Paul tells us who we fight against: the demonic forces of darkness that exist. When you and I are acting in accordance with God's will, we are impacting not only the earthly realm, but we are also impacting the spiritual realm; we are moving God's kingdom forward. Now conversely, if we do the works of darkness, we are pushing God's kingdom back on earth and we are strengthening the forces of darkness in the spiritual realm.

You think we have that much power? You better believe we have that much power. God created us to have authority and power! Have you ever asked, "Who does it hurt?" We think our actions effect only ourselves, but if we are a child of God acting in an ungodly way, it does great damage to the kingdom of God. We all once walked in ungodly ways and so we have done damage to the kingdom of God. Thank the LORD, when we repent, God forgives and forgets. Now, the people that witnessed our sin or were impacted by it, often that sin still stands in their minds.

When we are doing God's will, seeking His will, we are doing spiritual warfare and battling the forces of darkness. So, do you see why the enemy tries so hard to get us to sin and to walk away from God's will? We are pulling down his strongholds when we follow God. We are defeating his horde of demons and helping to set the captives free.

When we look at the LORD's Prayer, we need to see it as a prayer for God's redemption, His salvation, and the reestablishing of the relationship we were created to walk in. "<u>May Your peace come and may Your rule establish Your peace</u>." That's what the prayer is really saying.

I WILL BUILD MY CHURCH

At Philippi, which is north of the Sea of Galilee, Jesus established a very important principle for His Kingdom. He made the statement, *"On this rock I will build My Church."* [Matt. 16:18] The Hebrew word He used is *edah*, meaning the congregation of only those in the covenant community. We are more familiar with the Greek term *ekklesia*, which means "the called-out ones," usually translated as "the church."[108] Most scholars agree *edah* would have underlined Jesus' words. The second word in Hebrew that means assembly is *qahal*, which includes everyone in the land.[109]

There are several different things about the word *edah* that are very important. One is that it's related to the word *ed* which means "witness." When they talked about Israel coming together to form an army, they would refer to the *edah Yisrael*, the assembly of Israel. You see, they only used Israelites for the army. Now, I love this, the root word for *edah* is *ya'ad*, which means the "chosen" or "anointed one." This usually referred to the bride that was chosen by her husband. In a real sense, Jesus was saying, "I'm going to establish My covenant with My bride, My family, My followers." The principle is found in two pronouns in Matthew 16:18 that we often overlook. Look at it closely, *"On this rock **I** will build **My** Church."* The two pronouns are "**I**" and "**My**." Jesus was establishing that as the King, it is His Kingdom and His Church. He was also establishing His ownership, His authority, and His power behind it. Who is going to build it? "I will build My covenant community." This little statement is packed with meaning, authority, ownership, and the power that stands behind the Church!

In the "body" image Paul used for the Church, some are hands, some are feet, and all of the body members. But what about the head? Who is the head? Paul said it over and over, Jesus Christ, the Messiah is

---

[108] Stern, *Jewish NT Commentary*, p. 54; Matt. 16:18.
[109] Lois Tverberg, *Listening to the Language of the Bible: Hearing it Through Jesus' Ears*, ed. Bruce Okkema (Holland, MI: En-Gedi Resource Center, 2004), p. 106.

the head. [1 Cor. 12:12-31] In the human body, the head controls the whole body. If the connection between the brain and the muscles are severed, we say that person is disabled because either the brain can't send the message, the body can't receive the message, or the message is garbled. Jesus said, *"Without me you can do nothing,"* [John 15:5] because for the body to function, it must be properly connected to the head. When a church is nonfunctional or ineffective, they are possibly disconnected from their Head. <u>Jesus must always be the head!</u>

HIS GOOD NEWS

Jesus' message of the kingdom of God is included from Genesis through Revelation. It is the whole story; it is what we call the Good News of the Gospel. "Gospel" is an English word meaning "Good News." In Nazareth, Jesus read from Isaiah 61: *"The Spirit of the LORD is upon me for He has anointed me to preach the good news to the poor."* This Scripture is not talking about the physical condition of those in poverty. It is speaking of those who realize they don't have the power they need and are seeking God for it.

As we mentioned earlier, the Hebrew word for "good news" is *basar*. Here's the interesting thing: Isaiah called it "good news." That's the way it's translated. Jesus states it as the "good news." [Luke 4:18-19] The Hebrew word *basar* doesn't mean "good news." The word simply means "news" or "report."

Theoretically, how do we get good news? Very simple, *basa'* was almost exclusively used in one context, a military victory. When they won the battle, the report of the victory was called *basar*. It was also used to mean "report." We find "good news" used as a substitute for "gospel" in the Life Application Bible, The Amplified Bible, and God's Word Bible, to name a few. The Gospel is "The Good News." The *basar*, the Good News is, "God is winning the battle and has won the victory!" His kingdom has come and people are coming into freedom because of it. That is the Good News of the Gospel.

    Why is it good news? Jesus' interpretation is that God's kingdom is returning and the kingdom of darkness is being pushed back! God is winning the war! That's why it is good news to the poor. They realize that they can be set free! Set free from what? From addictions, a tormented mind, depression, self-doubt, and all the other things the enemy throws at us! Can you see, can you perceive how Jesus saw His Church? He saw His church breaking out into freedom, breaking the chains that bind them and leading those that will follow into freedom! Luke quotes Isaiah 61, *"Restoring sight to the blind,"* putting things back in order, setting captives free, binding up the broken hearted, and on and on! Reconciling and reestablishing God's order, restoring relationships, that's the Good News! God is undoing what was done to those who chose to believe in Him!

    That is the theme of Jesus' teachings and the reason He came. That is why He gave His disciples the message to go out and set the captives free. [Matt. 10:1] We have a choice! Which kingdom do we want to be a part of? Whatever kingdom we pick, the king becomes our father, and we will receive his inheritance. If God is our Father and King, we get His inheritance, but if Satan is our father and king, we get his inheritance. What did God say He had prepared for Satan and his angels? Hell, but it was not prepared for mankind.[110] But if we choose Satan as our father and king, we get his inheritance. It's just that simple. Most people would say, "I don't choose anyone." As I have said before and continue to say, there is not a third option. If you choose not to follow Jesus, not to be a part of the kingdom of God, you have chosen to follow Satan. That may sound harsh, but it is reality. God said, *"Today I have set before you life or death,"* **hint, hint,** *"therefore choose life."* [Deut. 30:19] God greatly desires for mankind to **choose life**.

Jesus came to give us life. We need to show people what God has done for us. Paul said we are *"to provoke them to jealousy."* [Rom. 11:11] We are to show the world that because of our relationship with the Living God through Jesus Christ, we have more peace, more joy, and more love in our lives. We want them to realize, "That's what I've been searching for all my life!"

There is a battle warring for the souls of mankind. Satan is the deceiver. He makes evil seem good and desirable. Like the fruit in the Garden, there is pleasure in sin for a season. But we all know, *"whatever a man sows, that he will also reap."* [Gal. 6:7] I often say, "We sow our wild seeds and then pray for crop failure." The first part of Galatians 6:7 says, *"Do not be deceived, God is not mocked!"* We may fool the world, but we can't fool

---

[110] See Nelson *NKJV Spirit Filled Bible*, Matt. 25:41b.

God!

Jesus proclaimed to Peter, *"On this rock, I will build My church,"* and He continued, *"and the gates of Hell will not prevail against it."* [Matt. 16:18] What are "the gates of Hell?" We should not look at this as an attack on the church. What do gates do? They keep people <u>out or in</u>. So, what was Jesus suggesting here? It seems clear to me. The gates of Hell hold people in bondage. **Jesus saw His church storming the gates of Hell and setting people free!**

When we break into freedom, Jesus expects us to storm those gates, pushing them back, so that those still in bondage can see the way out into freedom. What a joy it is to see someone set free from all the garbage Satan had used to keep them in chains. What a joy to see them walk into victory, and into God's peace. We are not to just escape into freedom only for ourselves! In the process of escaping, we are to bring others with us. After we have gained our freedom, we are to start the growing process. That was and still is Jesus' view of His church.

CHAPTER TEN

THE GREAT COMMANDMENT

BE MY DISCIPLES

What do you think Jesus thought was the most important thing that God said to man? *"Thou shall love the LORD thy God."* We call it the Great Commandment. Jesus said to the multitudes that were following Him, *"If anyone comes to Me and does not hate his father and mother, wife and children, brothers and sisters, yes, and his own life also, he cannot be My Disciple."* [Luke 14:25-27] Again, these seem like very harsh words and out of character for Jesus. We can see that this statement is in direct conflict with the fifth commandment, *"Honor your father and mother so that your days may be long."* [Exod. 20:12] This is the only commandment with promise.

Scripture tells us *"If someone says, 'I love God,' and hates his brother, he is a liar."* [1st John 4:20] If Jesus really meant "hate," then He had just advocated breaking God's Law! Jesus wouldn't do that! So, what was he really saying? He didn't mean 'hate' the way we think of hate. Here is why: In first century Hebrew, their vocabulary was small, so expressing certain concepts was difficult because there were no words to show comparison. For example, if you love someone but you love someone else more, there was no way in Hebrew to express that feeling. So the rabbis would use a radical expression, as the scriptures did. You love or you hate. Jesus was not advocating to hate because that would be the opposite of love. That would violate the nature of

God, the commandment of God, the message of Jesus, and 1 Corinthians 13. So, when Jesus said "hate," He was expressing a term of preference, in other words, "to love less."[111]

Another example of "to love less" is found in Malachi 1:2-3, *"Jacob I have loved, but Esau I have hated."* What the scripture was really saying was, "Jacob I love, Esau I love less." God chose Jacob over Esau because Jacob did not "despise his birthright," but sought the ways of the Lord. [Genesis 25:34] Esau despised his birthright and he didn't want the things of the LORD. In fact, Esau offended his family and God by marrying pagan women. That's why He said, "Jacob I love, Esau I love less." That is the love/hate issue. It is important to understand what it was saying in Hebrew. What Jesus meant by His statement found in Luke 14:25-27 was "If anyone is to be my disciple he is to love his father and mother less than…" He didn't finish His statement, but it's implied. Jesus was saying to us all, "You must love Me more than your father, mother, brother, sister, spouse and children, and even your own life." He was essentially saying what God was saying in the Great Commandment.

He said that His followers must *"take up his cross and follow Me."* [Matt. 16:24] Right? He was not talking about His own crucifixion. He uses crucifixion because it had become the most common form of execution during the occupation of Israel by the Roman Empire. The Romans developed crucifixion to humiliate the breakers of the law and suppress revolts. Rome was very cruel in their forms of execution. Judas of Gamala,

---

[111] Bivin, *New Light on the Difficult Words of Jesus*, p. 18.

the Galilean, lead a revolt in 6 A.D. against the Romans because of a census in Judea.[112] It is estimated that 98% of the revolts originated in the Galilee and most were over the issue of taxation. During the uprising associated with Judas of Gamala, around 2,000 people were crucified.[113]

The Judas of Gamala's revolt was crushed when Jesus was between the ages of nine and twelve. So during Jesus' childhood, He would have seen the Romans put down the revolt. They discouraged revolts in the Galilee region by lining the road leading to Sepphoris with literally thousands of crucified men, women, and children. Sepphoris was on top of the mountain above Nazareth.[114] Jesus used Sepphoris as His example of *"A city that is set on a hill that cannot be hidden."* [Matt. 5:14] That huge city's lights could be seen from any direction at night and its structures during the day.

Most of the people listening to Jesus had been touched by crucifixion either by witnessing one or by losing a loved one to it, so they knew what He meant when He said to take up his cross. Jesus was calling for His followers to stand for their faith against pagan opposition. So, what did Jesus mean? The condemned were required to carry their crossbeam to the place of crucifixion as part of the humiliation. They were carrying their own instrument of death. When Jesus said, "and follow Me," He meant that we must be willing to be so committed to Him and to His cause that

---

[112] Reader's Digest, *Atlas of the Bible* (New York: Reader's Digest, 1982), p. 174.
[113] Ibid., p. 176.
[114] Ibid., p. 176

we would be willing to die for our faith. That is what this statement means. He went on to tell His followers to count the cost of being one of His disciples before they committed. [Luke 14:28-33]

Does this sound easy? Jesus did not give them, or us, a cheap grace. Cheap grace does not exist! There is a high cost to being Jesus' disciple in the midst of a world that hates His message and His disciples. We are to live in a world that tempts us to give up the walk. It is a narrow road and a difficult one. Do you see why scripture tells us that we gain our *"salvation with fear and trembling?"* [Phil. 2:12] But Jesus promises us that we can walk in freedom. He tells us that it's not going to be easy. How different that is from what some have taught. Jesus was telling His followers of the first century and down through the ages that it's not easy, and the price is high, but the reward is eternal.

Just look at the original twelve disciples and Paul. They were despised, rejected, persecuted, stoned, imprisoned, and executed in horrid ways. In 64 A.D., while Rome burned, rumors spread that Emperor Nero had set fire to the city. To stop the rumors, he shifted the blame to the Christian community and they were put to death in many horrible ways, the most well-known being hung on poles and set on fire to light Nero's garden. A vast multitude of Christians were convicted, not of burning the city, but of "hating the human race."[115] Wow, did you realize that lie is that old? Outright persecution continued for hundreds of years. Emperor Domitian earned the reputation for

---

[115] Mark Galli, "Persecution in the Early Church: A Gallery of Persecution Emperors," in *Christian History Institute Magazine*, Issue 27, (1990): 137.

drinking the blood of saints, and Emperor Trajan is given the credit for throwing St. Ignatius to the lions in the coliseum.[116]

We are truly a blessed people to be able to worship our LORD openly. But there is still persecution for one's faith, Jews and Christians alike. People, especially missionaries, are still martyred daily. Ministers of the gospel around the world are beheaded in their pulpits and many are imprisoned unjustly. In America, if we stand on God's Word, if we stand for what is right in God's eyes, we are labeled as small-minded hate-mongers. Do you remember the shooting in 1999 at the Columbine High School? A student was asked if she believed in God, she answered "Yes!"[117] Like I said earlier, there is a high cost to walk after Him. <u>Are you willing to pay the price, if required?</u>

SH'MA

When Jesus asked His followers to commit everything to Him, it is the same as the Great Commandment. The account of the scribe questioning Jesus contains what we call the Great Commandment, and is found in Matthew 22:34-40, Mark 12:28-34, and Luke 10:25-29. There are slight variations in their accounts. As with any eye witness testimony, they remember different details, but they are basically saying the same thing.

---
[116] Ibid.
[117] Wikipedia, Cassie Bernall

145

We need to understand that it was the responsibility of the Sanhedrin to send out investigators to observe rabbis to see if they might be the Messiah. They wouldn't say anything, they would just observe. Remember the Pharisees and Sadducees that went out to observe John in Matthew 3:7? How many times in Scripture does it mention the Pharisees would be there observing, watching Jesus, and saying nothing? Then, if it seemed plausible that the person they were observing could be the Messiah, they would report back to the Sanhedrin what they had seen. The Sanhedrin would then send out teams to ask questions, to see how the person responded to all sorts of situations. So, the early testing was not meant to trick Jesus, but to see how He would respond and if He was possibly the Messiah. That was part of the process. Some of what went on later was meant to trick Him, but that was after they saw Jesus as a threat to their way of life.

So Jesus has just had a confrontation with the Sadducees, they were trying to trick him over whose wife a woman would be after death.[118] But He knew they didn't believe in the resurrection.[119] [Acts 23:8] After He answered them, a lawyer came up and asked a legitimate question. Jesus was a rabbi and it was common for rabbis to be asked questions. A lawyer was not a court lawyer, but a scribe, a teacher of the Law. This Lawyer came up to Jesus with respect and asked Him, *"Teacher, which is the great commandment in the law?"* [Matt. 22:36] "Commandment" in Hebrew is *mitzvah*.[120] He was asking Jesus for clarification. In

---

[118] Stern, *Jewish NT Commentary*, p. 66; verse 31-32.
[119] Ibid., p. 65; verse 24.
[120] Ibid., p. 96; verse 28.

other words, "Of all God's 613 Laws of Moses, what is the most important one?"

According to Luke, Jesus asked the lawyer the question back, which may have been exactly what happened. The other accounts had Jesus answering the lawyer's question. To the other writers, the lawyer wasn't important, so they recorded it as Jesus answering. Whether Jesus replied or the lawyer replied, it's still the same answer. It is very possible He used the rabbinical technique Question for Question, mentioned in the teaching on Jesus as a Boy.[121] Luke 2:46-47 tells us that when Jesus was twelve, *"they were amazed at His questions."*

So, what was His response? The best account of the response is recorded in Mark. Jesus answered him, *"Sh'ma Yisrael, Adonai Eloheynu, Adonai echad, V'ahavta et Adonai, l'vavcha, naphsh'kah m'odhekah."* [Mark 12:29-30] Jesus was a good Jew, He didn't use God's name, *Yahweh*, instead He said, *"Adonai."* In English, He said, *"Hear, O Israel, the* LORD *our God, the* LORD *is one. You shall love the* LORD *your God with all your heart, with all your soul, and with all your strength."* That was the way He began. Why is that important? Primarily because *sh'ma*, in Hebrew, which technically means "hear," but, it actually has three levels of meaning as we mentioned earlier.

My favorite illustration of *sh'ma* is a child misbehaves and the parent begins giving correction. Halfway through, they might say something like, "Do you hear me?" There are three levels of meaning in this question. The Greek word that matches this is *akouo*,

---

[121] Phelps, *Hidden Treasures Revealed*, Part 1, p. 35-36.

which we get the word "acoustic" from "to hear." It's used in the same three ways. Now the first level of understanding on the surface is: Do you hear me; are you listening to me; do you perceive the sound of my voice? The second level is: Do you understand what I am saying? The parent wants to know that the child not only hears the words, but understands what is being said. The third level is the key, it is obedience. "Are you going to do what I say?"

Let me tell you what happened in 1 Samuel 15. Saul was sent out to the battlefield with a command from God to utterly destroy the enemy and take nothing from them: no cattle, or wealth, or any of their possessions. But in 15:8, it says, *"So, Saul and the people spared Agag and the best of the sheep."* King Saul knew he was supposed to have killed him. When the Prophet Samuel arrived, Saul said, *"I have performed the commandment of the LORD. But Samuel said, what then is this bleating of the sheep in my ear, and the lowing of oxen which I hear?"* Saul said, *"We did everything God said, we killed everything. However, the best of their cattle and the best of their sheep we kept to offer a 'sacrifice to the LORD your God.'"* Saul blamed the people for taking the plunder for a sacrifice. Samuel replied, *"Has the LORD as great delight in burnt offerings and sacrifices, as in obeying the voice of the LORD?"* He was saying, "Do you not know that obedience is better than sacrifice?" Why would God give a command and then be pleased because His command was disobeyed?

Guess what the word "obey" is in that text? *Sh'ma*! To hear, to understand, and to obey.[122] God says

---

[122] Nelson, *The Exhaustive Concordance*, p. 145; Hebrew word #8085.

plainly here that obedience is better than any sacrifice. You see, we find it repeatedly in the scripture. In *Strong's Concordance* and others, s*h'ma* shows up for obey and obedience, and yet it means to hear. So, it literally means intelligent listening for the purpose of understanding and responding. *Sh'ma* (hear) *Yisrael* (Israel), *Adonai Eloheynu* (the LORD our God), *Adonai echad* (The LORD is one). Now, what does this set up? In Deuteronomy, God was getting ready to give the Ten Commandments and the other commands to Moses. God was saying, "I am getting ready to give you a command Israel. I want you to hear it, to understand it, and I expect you to do it."

YOU SHALL LOVE

The very next thing that He said was, "*V'ahavta et Adonai,*" or *"You shall love."* We could actually say, "You must love." My feeling is God rightfully expects us to *"love the* LORD *your God."* Look at all He has done for us and the only expectation He has is that we love the LORD our God completely.

What do we normally think of love as? We think of it as an emotion that we can fall into and fall out of. My definition of the way the world sees love is: someone walking along, falling into a hole, and then climb out! I can't say that love has nothing to do with emotion because it has a lot to do with emotions. But, by definition, the Jewish understanding of love is not primarily or predominantly an emotion. It does consist of passion, to a greater or lesser degree, depending on how strong the love is; the stronger the love, the greater the passion and it should never be deemphasized. Love, in the Jewish understanding, is predominantly an action word, a verb. It does not describe a feeling, it has a broad range of meanings, but the proof of love is always in its demonstration. Love is never generic, it is never without an object, it is always in a specific relationship, and it is a relational term.

Love is the language of the Covenant, but what love means here is to value one another. Stop and think about that for a moment. The more we love, the more we value, right? Someone that we love greatly, we value highly. The one we love the most is number one on our priority list because they have a higher importance to us. So, when Jesus says, *"And you shall love,"* the verse is actually saying, "I'm going to establish that God will be of highest priority." Why does He expect God to be of highest value? Because God deserves it. He is our Creator, our Heavenly Father, and our Savior. It is the most important relationship– a life and death relationship! So, *"You shall love the Lord your God."* and He goes on to say, *"with all..."* It's another way of saying, "more than," just like Jesus put God first. More than, means with every part of our heart. We are to value God more, and that's the whole process. Valuing God above everything, it's God's command, it's not an emotion.

No one can command an emotion because emotions are reactions. Do you see why is it wrong to be ruled by emotions, to let that which is designed to be a response become ruler? People have ruined their lives by reacting to situations and making irrational responses; their emotions took over. The emotions in our lives are there to serve us, not to rule over us. Therefore, if the emotion of anger, fear, or jealousy are ruling a life, it is out of order.

Love is a way of dealing with someone because we value them. God tells Israel, "I want you to value Me so much that you will prize My way above your way or anything you possess. I am to be considered the most important thing in your life. When you do that, everything else, all the rest of your relationships will fall into place." When we put God first in our lives, He expands our ability to love others more. When our children were little, my wife, Diann, once told God, "God I love You, but I can't imagine loving You more than John or our children." When our lives changed in 1985, she was able to put God first, and He increased her capacity to love beyond her imagination. Putting God first does not diminish our love for others, it increases it. I was telling someone that and they had a good way of putting it, "It is like in *The Grinch That Stole Christmas*, when the Grinch's heart tripled in size, only our hearts in real life." In our way of thinking, that doesn't seem possible, but I can testify it is the truth. He expands our ability to love.

Don't ever put family or work above God, and don't put work above your family. If God is the number one relationship, then what would God want our number two relationship to be? Our Family because it is the second longest relationship we're going to have. We leave father and mother and cling to our mate because the two are to become one, as with God. This relationship is meant to last until the end of our days. It is the second most important relationship. Now, after family, our next priority may be a ministry or job, or church.

When we get our priorities out of order, we are out of balance. God once showed me to order our priorities according to their longevity. That which is most important should be that which lasts the longest: God, number one; family, number two; ministry or career is for a season, so that should be number three. It goes on down the line. Deuteronomy 6:5 is saying, "Order your relationships with God as number one."

ALL YOUR HEART

L'vavcha, or *"with all your heart,"* is another way of saying, "with all your mind." In the Jewish understanding, heart did not mean a physical organ, it meant with all the produce of our heart: the seat of intelligence, our thoughts, our will, our ideas about how things ought to be done. It's another word for what we call the mind today.

We now know that the mind is more than just the brain, or the seat of intelligence. There is a consciousness, awareness, and association that is more than just the sum of its parts. So, the whole mental emotional will of a person: decisions, choices, ideas, intelligence, and plans- these are all part of the activity of the heart. In this verse, "with all your heart," Jesus presented it as, "<u>God is more important than our understanding, our ideas, our will, or what we think</u>.

So, when God says love and we get angry, we

are choosing our will over His. The first time I realized that was when my wife and I were having a discussion punctuated with heated emotion. We were arguing, and the trouble was she was right, but I didn't want to accept it because I knew it was something I should have been doing and hadn't. She was often God's voice to me and I didn't like it. I went stomping out of the house, and was walking up the hill to the church. Oh boy, was I angry. I got to the end of the sidewalk and I heard a voice and I knew who it was. It was God. He said, "Why are you so angry?" I began, "Well, she said..." In the middle of that, He cut me off and said, "You're angry because you're choosing to be! You're choosing to let anger rule you. You could just as easily choose that it's not that important. You could choose that the relationship is more important than what you are feeling and decide that it's not worth the conflict!" Oh my, I didn't want to hear that, but He was right. For the first time in my life I realized that <u>anger is a choice</u>. When anger comes up, I choose whether it is going to rule me or I rule it. If I let it rule me, it governs my words and my actions causing me to give in to my emotions. Whether it is anger, fear, frustration, or impatience, we have a choice. For the first time, I realized God was teaching me about love.

I want to share with you the translation of 1st Corinthians 13 according to John Phelps, starting with verse 4: "Love **chooses to** be patient. Love **chooses to** be kind. Love **chooses not to** keep a record of wrong. Love **chooses to** forgive." I can only forgive with God's help. <u>Choosing to forgive is not an emotion, it is a choice</u>. I choose forgiveness over woundedness or unforgiveness! To be patient with you, I choose that you are more important than my frustration. We must value the person more than we value our feelings. It is always a choice. So, when we are making choices, we need to choose to let God's will rule over our will!

That is what it means to, *"Love God with all your heart."* God has a plan for our lives, for your life, but we all have a choice. So, let's all choose God's plan rather than our plan. If God has something He wants you to do, and you don't want to do it, choose to do it God's way rather than your way. Make the choice in every situation to let God be first, rather than your way. Submit to His authority, yield, and let God rule. That's how you make God first in your heart. Yes, that sounds foreign to most of us, but oh what joy we find when we let Him rule!

ALL YOUR SOUL

The second part of *"And you shall love"* is, *nephesh, "with all your soul."* The Jewish understanding of the soul is our life essence, our identity, our very being. It's not just being alive, it is the quality of our life, of who we are. I define it as our personality, the "who" of who we are. It's specific, the essence of what makes us, us. God wants us to love Him more than our personality and our identity. If God says, "I want to change this aspect of you," don't say, "But that's the way I have always been." If you love God more, then you will say, "God, You can do whatever You want. "Change my heart, O Lord" means, "Change my mind, change my attitude," but, "Change my soul" means, "Change my identity, my very being." When we allow God to change us, we find we like ourselves so much more.

Scripture says the soul and the spirit can only be divided by God's two-edged sword. [Heb. 4:12] The spirit is what we are, the soul is who we are, and the body is where the soul and spirit are housed. The soul is our identity; it is our very life-being. Our goal should be to love God more than our soul, which means that we do not prize our personality or our ways of being more than God. This is not easy, but when we truly desire that closer walk with God, it is required. God wants to "refine us, what is good will be better, what is bad will be eliminated."[123] Loving God with all my soul implies that kind of commitment.

It is the soul that is redeemed. That means that what we carry into the age to come is that spiritual reality linked with our identity. We do not lose our individuality or identity when we move from this age into the next. We do not merge, as the Eastern Mystics say, into a cosmic oomph where everyone loses their identity and just becomes part of the whole. We don't move into Nirvana which is really the cessation of everything, blankness, into a universe where we lose consciousness. No, Christianity and Judaism believe that we will retain our identity. The soul is our very life essence, our being, connected to the spirit. <u>When we accept Jesus as our Savior and LORD, our soul belongs to God.</u> He saves our soul, He delivers our personality, our life, and our being from destruction.

---

[123] See Nelson's *NKJV Spirit Filled Bible*, p. 1386; Malachi 3:1-3.

ALL YOUR STRENGTH

The last one is, *"with all our strength."* This is a strange one. M*e*od is not a noun, it is an adverb. It translates, "with all your very" or "with all your much."[124] That doesn't make much sense to us, does it? This is a very unique structure in Hebrew. It means, "With all your much-ness." We could say, "With all your passion" or, "with all your stuff that you possess." With all our skills and abilities and gifts. With all our reputation or our position at work, or our role as a wife and mother, or husband, father, friend, or a counselor. Yes, all the stuff that makes up our lives, all the very-ness and much-ness of our lives. None of this can be more important than God. Not the things we possess, the things we're able to do, our skills and abilities, or our strengths. Nothing is more important than God. Now, this covers everything; everything is covered by the Great Commandment. We give Him our intelligence, our will, our emotion, our very personality, and life-being. When we give Him all the things we possess and that makes up our lives, nothing is left accept the spirit, which belongs to God. The Spirit returns to God, who sends it.

So, what did Paul say about the body? Our bodies are corrupted because of our appetites. He said, *"Present your body as a living sacrifice."* [Rom. 12:1] The terms Paul used here refers to the offerings at the Temple. What happens to the offering in the Temple? It is burned up! Who does it belong to when it is offered? It belongs to God. What Paul was saying was that we

---

[124] Strong, *The Exhaustive Concordance*, p. 70; Hebrew word #3966.

are to make our bodies a living sacrifice to the LORD. We must bring our lives under His authority and bring discipline into our lives.

Understand that the body must be brought under submission. We choose to make the sacrifice and give it all to the LORD. We renew our mind by not being conformed in the old life, but by being transformed into the new way of thinking, into a mindset that is wholly and acceptable to God. We have a new foundation, new standards, new priorities, and new values. Based on those new values, they will affect how we see things, how we make decisions, and how we live our lives.

LOVE YOUR NEIGHBOR

What does the world say? Look after yourself. What does God say? Love others. Jesus said, *"You shall love the LORD your God with all your heart, soul, and strength,"* and *"Love your neighbor as yourself."* [Matt. 22:37-40] This is another one of what I like to call the coin principle. We cannot have one side without the other. Jesus was saying that if you love God, you will love others. It is stated clearly: *"If someone says, 'I love God,' and hates his brother, he is a liar."* [1st John 4:20] We cannot love God without loving others. If we put God as number one in our life, we are going to do what He says, and He says, "Love your brother." If we don't love our brother, then we are not making God number one in our lives. Do you see the inconsistency here? We are not loving Him with all our heart, soul and strength. It's just that simple. We cannot truly love our neighbor the way God intends without loving God first. That's why Jesus said the First Commandment is to love God totally and the second is similar. He wasn't saying there is a second principle, he was saying that it is the other side of the first, and we are back to the coin principle.

How do we know it's the other side? What does Paul tell us and what does James tell us that lets us know that loving others is indicative that loving God is in place? If you really fulfill the royal Law according to the Scripture, what do you do? He said something very specific: *"Love your neighbor as yourself. In doing so you keep the royal Law."* [James 2:8] And Paul says, *"For all of the Law is fulfilled in one word, even in this; You shall love your neighbor as yourself."* [Gal. 5:14] Paul was stating that when we love our neighbor as ourselves, we are keeping the whole of the Law.

It is impossible to wholly and completely love another without the love of God in us. The world's kind of love is possessive, jealous, and self-centered. It says, "I will love you as long as you please me, make me happy, satisfy my desires," and so on. We cannot love others the way we should unless our love for God is what it is supposed to be. If we don't love God the way we are supposed to, then we are sitting on the throne of our lives, not God. If I'm most important, I cannot love you the way I'm supposed to. When I love God more than myself, then I'm able to love you properly. This makes no sense to the world. The world says, "Take care of number one; put yourself first." Even the person with self-hatred or low self-esteem attention is centered on self. See the self in both terms? It's a trap; either way we go, too high or too low, it still puts self at the center of our world. <u>To be free and to love completely, we must submit to God, and He will increase our capacity to love.</u>

That's why marriages that do not put God first are in for all sorts of problems. Their actions will be predicated on "me, my wants, and my needs." When couples come to me for premarital counseling, I tell them, "You've heard that marriage is give and take. That is wrong, because the minute you say, 'I've given all I'm going to give, it's my turn to get.' Then the marriage is in big trouble." Marriage is literally give, because if both people are committed to giving, each will be receiving what he/she needs. Problems occur when party one gives and party two receives, and party two only gives when it's in their interest. We can be kind to someone if we're going to get something back. In stating, "Love your neighbor as yourself," Jesus was saying, "If you love only those that love you, how different is that from the world? That's what pagans do." They love people that love them, because there's something in it for them. To love someone that is unlovable, to love for the sake of loving, now, that's a challenge, but it is what God expects.

What did Paul tell us about brotherly love? *"giving preference to one another."* [Rom. 12:10] What is the foundational principle of relationships? Love is the primary principle that is the foundation of it all. 1st John tells us "God is love." What does Jesus say the characteristic of His disciples would be? *"So, that all men will know you are my disciples, that you will have love one for another."* [John 13:35] Jesus called His disciples, and all His followers, to a higher standard. *"A new commandment I give to you, that you love one another; as I have loved you."*

[John 13:34-35] Do you see, Jesus just kicks it up to another level? How did Jesus show His love? He died for our sins.

The comparison He shares with us here is the demonstration of love. If you do not demonstrate love to your brother then how can you say you love God? Love is always shown in demonstration! So, if you do not choose to love others, then what makes you think that you really love God? That's the bottom line of this. When Jesus said, "Love Me more," He was really saying, "This is the same as the Great Commandment." God is saying that for your relationships to be in right order, He has to be honored and preferred above all else. Value Him and His way first, and He will show you how to put the rest of your life in proper order.

All 613 Laws deal with our relationship with God, our relationship with others, or what our relationship should be with ourselves.[125] We are to love ourselves, because how can we love our brother if we don't love ourselves? We are told to love our neighbor as our self. God knows that love of self is a given. God tells us to put Him first and He will put us on the proper path.

Here is an interesting statement that God gave me. He said, "If Jesus didn't put you here, what are you doing here? If Jesus did put you here, what are you doing here?" In other words, if Jesus puts us in certain situations, then we must decide what we are going to do. Are we loving, are we being His representatives? And if He didn't put us there, then what are we doing there in the first place? The point is, if we let God put us

---

[125] Cohen, *Everyman's Talmud*, p. 146-158.

where He wants us, man, lookout because His blessings are coming!

Do you know why it's safer to trust God then to trust in yourself? Remember, *"Trust in the LORD with all your heart and lean not in your own understanding; in all your ways acknowledge Him, and He will direct your path."* [Prov. 3:5-6] I don't know what's coming tomorrow, but He does! I have determined that whatever tomorrow holds, *"as for me and my house, we will serve the LORD."* [Josh. 24:15] We often make bad decisions because, at that moment, it looked good, but we don't know what tomorrow will bring. If we could only learn to check in with God first, and wait for His answer.

The whole point is being able to trust God more than our own perception, more than our own interpretation, more than our intelligence, more than our own abilities, and our own awareness. Even with all of our intellect, we are flawed and limited in our understanding. But God has perfect knowledge and understanding! Putting ourselves in His hands is the safest place we can ever be. As a servant of the LORD's, I can say it is also the scariest because when we give God control, we must **"let go and let God."** Most of us are control freaks, so trusting God for our eternal destination is no biggie, but trusting Him about who we should marry, what job to take, or how to spend our money, is very foreign for most of us. Giving God true Lordship of our lives will set us free to love and trust God with all our heart and soul and to love our neighbors as ourselves.

"Eastern Gate"

John's sources came from many years of research; however, we have done our best to provide resources for our readers, in hopes to encourage further research. With the advantages of technology today, much of this information can be found on the internet.

SELECTED BIBLIOGRAPHY

Bivin, David and Roy Blizzard. *Understanding the Difficult Words of Jesus*. Shippensburg, PA: Destiny Image Publishers, 1994.

Bivin, David. *New Light on the Difficult Words of Jesus: Insights from His Jewish Context*. Holland, MI: En-Gedi Resource Center, 2005.

Cohen, Abraham. *Everyman's Talmud: The Major Teachings of the Rabbinic Sages*. New York, NY: Schocken, 1995.

Edersheim, Alfred. *The Temple: Its Ministry and Services, as They Were at the Time of Jesus*. London: The Religious Tract Society, 1881.

------. *Sketches of Jewish Life in the Days of Christ*. London: The Religious Tract Society, 1876.

Flusser, David. *Jesus*. Reinbeck: Rowohlt, 1968.

Galli, Mark. "Persecution in the Early Church: A Gallery of Persecution Emperors." In *Christian History Institute Magazine*, Issue 27, (1990).

Garrard, Alec. *The Splendor of the Temple*. Grand Rapids, MI: Kregel Publications, 2001.

Gehman, Henry Snyder and John D. Davis. *The New Westminster Dictionary of the Bible*. Westminster: Westminster Place, 1970.

Goldenberg, Robert. *The Jewish Quarterly Review* 92, no.

¾ (2002): 568-88.
Howard, Kevin and Marvin Rosenthal. *The Feasts of the Lord*. Winter Garden, FL: Zion's Hope, 1996.
Josephus, Flavius. *Josephus, the Essential Writings: A Condensation of Jewish Antiquities and the Jewish War*. Translated and edited by Paul L. Maier. Grand Rapids, MI: Kregel Publications, 1988.
Lightfoot, John. *A Commentary on the New Testament from the Talmud and Hebraica: Matthew- 1 Corinthians*. Vol. 2. Grand Rapids: Baker Book House, 1979.
Lindsey, Robert L. *Jesus, Rabbi & Lord: The Hebrew Story of Jesus Behind Our Gospels*. New Orleans: Cornerstone Publishers, 1990.
Moseley, Ron. *Yeshua: A Guide to the Real Jesus and Original Church*. Clarksville, MD: Messianic Jewish Publishers, 1998.
Murphy, Frederick J. *Early Judaism: The Exile to the Time of Jesus*. Peabody, MA: Hendrickson Publishers, 2002.
Phelps, John. *Hidden Treasures Revealed: Teaching the Jewish Roots of the Christian Faith, Part One*. haOr l' Olam Ministry, 2016
Reader's Digest. *Atlas of the Bible*. New York: Reader's Digest, 1982.
Safrai, Samuel and M. Stern. *The Jewish People in the First Century: Historical Geography, Political History, Social, Cultural and Religious Life and Institution*. Assen: Van Gorcum, 1974.
Stern, David H. *Jewish New Testament Commentary: A Companion Volume to the Jewish New Testament*. Clarksville, MD: Jewish New Testament Publications, 1992.
Strassfield, Michael. *The Jewish Holidays: A Guide and*

Commentary. New York: Harper & Row, 1985.
Strong, James. *The Exhaustive Concordance of the Bible*. Cincinatti: Jennings & Graham, 1890.
------. *New Strong's Exhaustive Concordance*. Nashville: Thomas Nelson, 2003.
Tenney, Merrill C. *The Zondervan Pictorial Bible Dictionary*. 25th ed. Grand Rapids: Zondervan, 1963.
Tverbeg, Lois. *Listening to the Language of the Bible: Hearing it Through Jesus' Ears*. Edited by Bruce Okkema. Holland, MI: En-Gedi Resource Center, 2004.
Young, Brad H. *Jesus the Jewish Theologian*. Grand Rapids, MI: Baker Publishing Group, 1993.

Ancient Semitic Alphabets

(With modern Hebrew, in column at right, for comparison)

Inscr. of Dibon. 9th. cent. B.C. Gen. §§ 1,2	Phoenician Coins and Inscript.	New-Punic.	Old. Hebr. Coins and Gems.	Samaritan.	Aram.-Egyptian. 5th.—1st. cent. B.C.	Palmyra Inscript. 1st sect. B.C. —4th. cent. A.C.	Heb. Inscr. Christ's Time.	Square Char.	Raschi.	Modern Hebrew	
✦✦	✦✦✦	✗	✦✦✦✦	✦✦	✦✦✦✦	α א	ʌ א	א	ᚆ	א	ʼ
𝟡𝟡	𝟡𝟡𝟡	𝟡,'	𝟡𝟡𝟡	𝟡	𝟡𝟡𝟡'	𝟡𝟡	בב	ב	ג	ב	b, bh
٦٦	ʌʌʌ	ʌʌ	ʌ٦٦	⊤	ʌ ʌ	ʌ ʌ		ג	ג	ג	g, gh
◁△	△◁△	𝟡,ι	△𝟡△𝟡	ᚎ	𝟡𝟡𝟡	𝟡𝟡	ד ד	ד	ד	ד	d, dh
∃∃	∃∃∃	∃	∃∃∃∃	ᚎ	∩∩∩∩	ᚆ ה	ה ה	ה	ה	ה	h
ΥΥ	٩٩٩	٩	٩٩٩٩	٭٭	٩٩٩١١	٦٩٩	١١ι	ו	ו	ו	w
⊥	⤴⤵⍉	⤷⌐	⤴⦕⥅⦖	ᚎ ⧸⧸	⎮ ⎮	⎮⎮	ז	ז	ז	ז	z
HHH	ARA	R,u	⤴⤵⤷⤸	⤷⤸ᚎ	∩∩∩∩⤷⤸	ᚆᚆ	ᚆ∩	ח	ח	ח	ch
	⊖⊖	⊖⊖		⤷ᚆ⤸	⊖⊖⊖⊖⊖	⊖⊖		ט	ט	ט	t
⟂⟂	ᚆᚎᚆᚎ	⟂⟂	⟂⟂ᚆᚎ	ᚎ⤷	ᚎᚎ⟂∣∣∣∣	ᚎᚎᚎ⦾	٦٦	'	.	"	y
ΨΨ	٦٦٦٦	ΨΨ	٦٦٦	ᚎᚎ	٦٦٦٦	ᚎ⦏ᚎ	ככ	ך כ	ד כ	ך כ	k, kh
66	∠∠∠∠	⌐	⌊⌊⌊⌊	2∠	∠∠∠∠∣	⌊⌊	⌊⌊	ל	ל	ל	l
ΨΨ	⟋⟍⟍	⋈×	⟋⟍ΨΨ	⌐⌐⌐	⌐⌐⌐⌐⌐	⌐⌐⌐	⟍⊖	מ ם	מ ם	מ ם	m
⅃⅃	⅃⅃⅃	⏐⏐	⅃⅃⅃⅃	⌐⌐⌐⌐	⅃⅃⅃⅃⌐	∣⅃	J	נ ן	נ ן	נ ן	n
⊕⊕	⤷⤸⤹⦾	⥊	⦏⦐	⤷⤹⤹⦏⦐⦏⦐		⌐⌐	⤷⤹	ס	ס	ס	s
∘	∘∘∪∪	∘᛫	∘∘∘∘	∘∘	∪∪ΥΥ	ʋ	ʋʋ	ע	ע	ע	ʻ
⅃⅃	⅃⅃⅃	⅃⅃	ʃ	⊐⊐⅃⅃⅃⅃	⅃⅃	⊐⅃	פ ף	פ ף	פ ף	p, ph
⤷⤸	⤷⤸⤹⦑	⦑⦒	⦑⦒⤷⤸⅃⅃	⤸⦎⦏	⦑⦒	⦑⦒	⤹	ץ צ	צ ץ	צ ץ	ṣ
ΡΡΡ	ΥΥΥ	⊤Ρ	⊤ΡΡ	⊤ΡΡ	⊤ΡᚆΡ	⌐	Ρ	ק	ק	ק	q
99	999	9,ι	999	999991	ΥΥΥ	⌐⌐	⌐	ר	ר	ר	r
ww	wwww	ᚆᚆ	www	∞ω	ΨΨΨ	ΨΨ	ΨΨ	שׁשׂ	שׁשׂ	ש	sh
×	⌐⌐⥀⥀	⌐⌐	+×+	×ʌ	⦎⦏	⤷⤸	⤷⤸	ת	ת	ת	t

INDEX

Adonai, 146, 148
Aesop's Fables, 66
ahavah, 73
aionios, 104
akouo, 129, 146
angelos, 10
Anno Domini, 7
Apocrypha, 64
Ascetic Jew, 106
basar, 109, 136
bet midrash, 77
Christ, 3, 37, 53, 102, 104, 124, 128
circumlocution, 17, 20, 24
Constantine, 38
derash, 70, 71, 72, 73
echad, 146, 148
edah, 134, 135
ekklesia, 134
Elijah, 34, 86
Eloheynu, 146, 148
emunah, 128
Essenes, 75, 80, 81, 82
Gan Eden, 19
ginosko, 126, 127
Hillel, 9, 67, 68, 82
Hinnom, 19
Israel, 8, 10, 16, 38, 40, 64, 77, 80, 82, 88, 94, 95, 102, 121, 135, 141, 146, 148, 150

Judah, 7, 122
Judea, 7, 142
katallasso, 102, 126
keruvim, 12
Kethuvim, 105
kharut, 72
kherut, 72
Kosher, 39
l'vavcha, 146, 151
Maccabees, 64, 75, 79
mal'ak, 10
meditate, 94
M^eod, 155
Messiah, 6, 15, 19, 27, 29, 31, 34, 37, 40, 44, 70, 73, 80, 87, 102, 106, 107, 128, 129, 135, 145
metanoia, 53
midrash, 65, 66, 70, 71, 72, 73
mikveh, 43
Mount Moriah, 7
nephesh, 153
netzer, 73
Nevi'im, 105
notzri, 73
outer garment, 39
p'rushim, 75
p'shat, 69
Palestine, 38
Passover, 9, 94, 95
Pentecost, 9, 53

Pharisees, 6, 69, 75, 76, 77, 79, 81, 98, 99, 101, 145
poosh, 35
poretz, 34
Prophesy, 38
Pseudepigrapha, 64
publicans, 55, 56
qahal, 135
Question for Question, 146
rabbi, ix, 9, 34, 46, 48, 66-69, 71, 72, 75, 79, 82-86, 88, 94, 103, 140, 145
remez, 69, 70
Sabbath, 1, 76, 98, 99
Sadducees, 75, 79, 80, 99, 145
Samaria, 7, 41
Sanhedrin, 78, 100, 123, 145
saw-far, 81
Sepphoris, 142
Septuagint, 16, 127
seraphim, 13
sh'ma, 129, 146-148
shaba, 11, 12
Shabbat, 12, 38, 41, 77, 98
shalom, 106, 130
shamayim, 18, 22

Shammai, 9, 67, 82
sod, 73, 74
sozo, 46
Synagogue, 1, 3, 4, 10, 41, 43, 44, 46, 48, 77, 106
tallit, 38
talmidim, 82
Talmud, 65, 78, 82, 93, 116
Tanakh, 105
Tesh'uvah, 53
Torah, 41, 78, 105
tzitzit, 39
tzitziyot, 39, 74
ya'ad, 135
Ya'ir, 44, 45
Yahweh, 146
yasha, 47, 49
Yeshua, 5, 19, 31, 47, 71, 77, 102, 114, 119, 122, 132
yetzer ha-ra, 71
yetzer hatov, 71
YHWH, 20, 74
Yisrael, 135, 146, 148
yod, 71
yodah, 126, 127
Zakkai, 54, 55, 56, 57
Zealots, 75, 81, 82
zoe, 104

Made in the USA
Columbia, SC
24 May 2019